PURELY CLASSIC RECIPES

22 delicious recipes

THE PURELY TWINS

Published in the United States.
By Purely Twins, LLC, Charlotte, NC.

Purely Classic Recipes
Copyright © 2012 by Lori Morris and Michelle Corso
Photography © 2012 by Lori Morris and Michelle Corso
All rights reserved. No part of this book may be reproduced in any form, without written permission from the authors.

Find us on facebook, twitter and pinterest.
http://www.facebook.com/purelytwins
http://www.twitter.com/purelytwins
http://www.pinterest.com/purelytwins

Follow us on instagram:
http://www.instagram.com/purelymichelle
http://www.instagram.com/purelylori
Check out our videos on fitness and healthy cooking onYouTube:
http://www.youtube.com/pure2rawtwins

Visit us online to find more about us at our blog. You will find allergy friendly and low sugar recipes and tips on health and fitness at http://purelytwins.com.

Luckiest Guy Font Design by Brian J. Bonislawsky DBA Astigmatic (AOETI)

DEDICATION

To our family,
for the lifetime of love, support, encouragement, faith, and strength. This cookbook could not have been done without your belief in us!

"We hope this cookbook brings a smile to your face, happiness into your kitchen, and joy to your life. We are honored and excited to share our classic sweet favorites with you."

~ Michelle and Lori, the Purely Twins

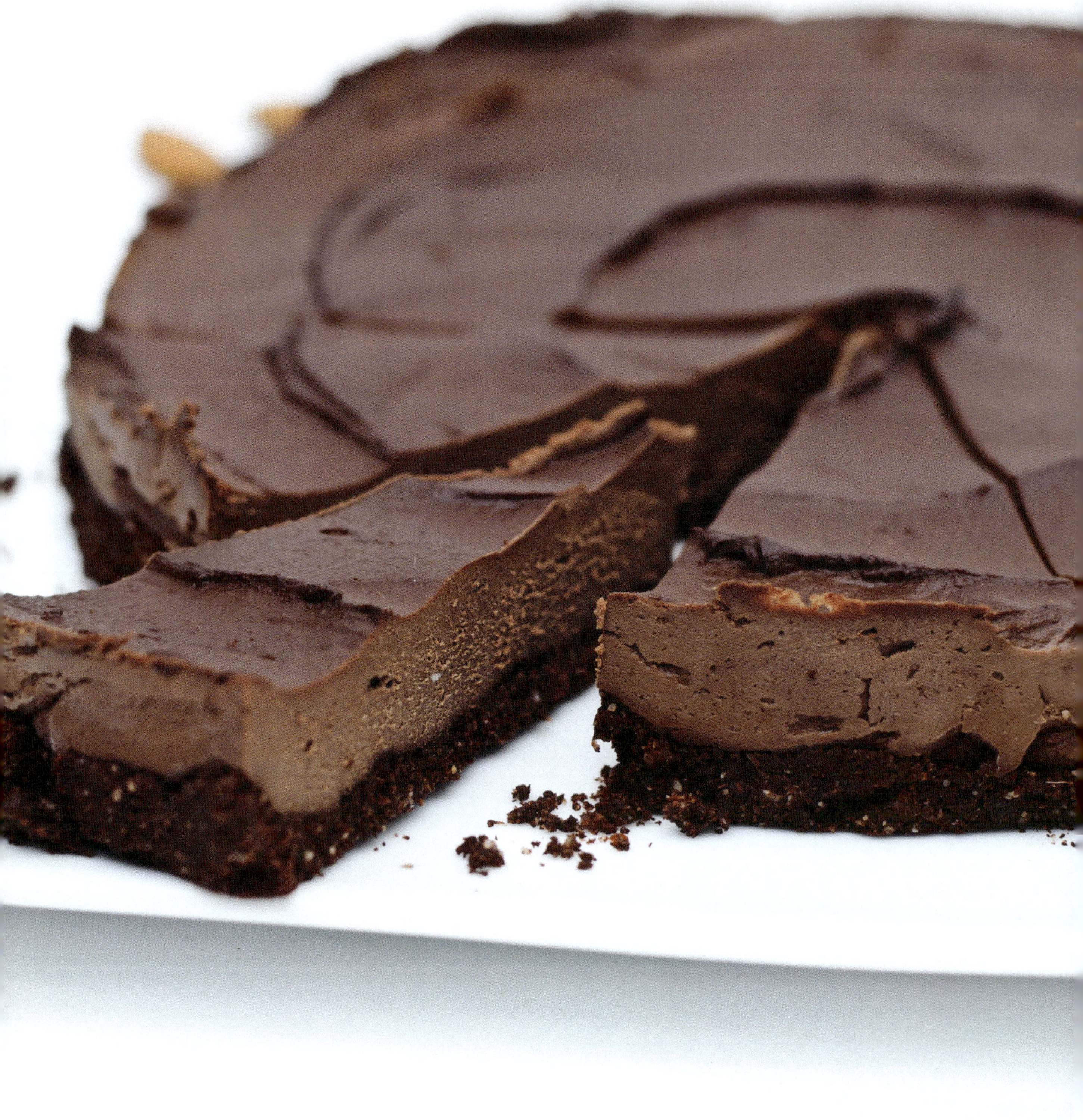

PURELY LOVE

We are Lori and Michelle, twin sisters who have a passion for baking. We are the creators of the blog *purelytwins.com* and recipe developers for this cookbook. This is our very first cookbook highlighting our favorite classic recipes, some from our blog and some from our time as bakery owners. It's a collection of gluten-free and vegan recipes, with options to make them customized to your taste.

We want to show that eating gluten-free can still be tasty and healthy. This collection of recipes showcases our love of food from pancakes to frostings to truffles. You will find a mix of raw and baked recipes! We hope to share our love of food with you through our recipes that you can re-create in your own kitchen.

We are huge dessert lovers. Not only do we get the joy in eating our recipes ourselves, but love sharing them with others, too. We have worked hard putting this cookbook together. Lots of time and dirty dishes. And of course enjoyed our yummy sweet treats along the way.

We hope you take pleasure in making our favorites as much as we do. We have provided full color photos throughout, recipe substitutions, and a resource page of ingredients and kitchen tools.

Happy baking from one dessert lover to another!

Find more about us at our blog http://purelytwins.com.

Love,
Lori & Michelle

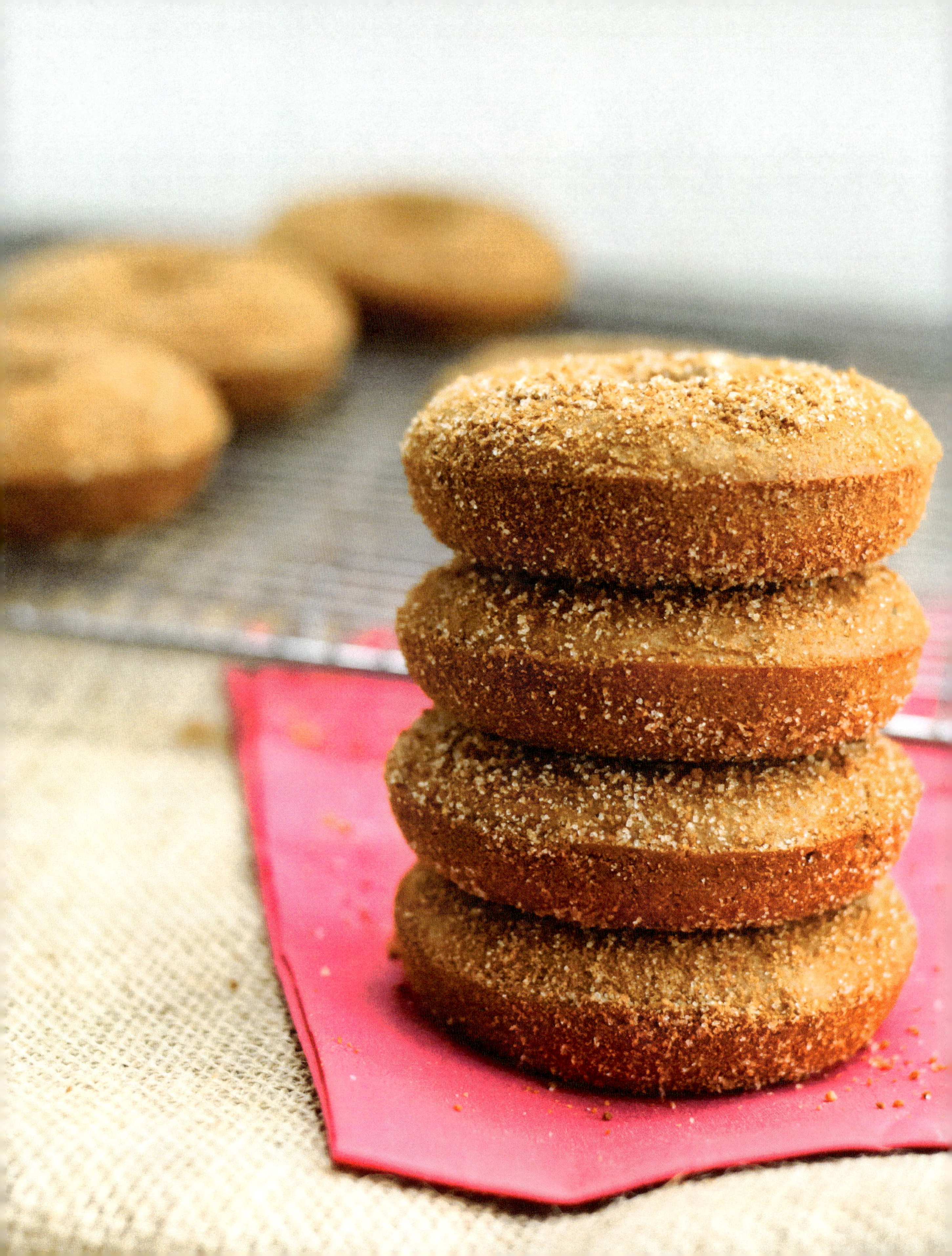

RECIPES YOU WILL FIND IN THIS COOKBOOK

Buttermilk pancakes
Baked donuts
Individual carrot cakes
Lemon blueberry scones
Fudgy brownies
Chocolate chip cookies
Almond cardamom biscotti
Cashew coconut biscotti
Mesquite cocoa biscotti
Cashew nib dough balls
Spiced cocoa dough balls

Key Lime pudding
Chocolate date macaroons
Protein thin mints
Coco thin mints
Chocolate cream cake
Low-sugar cocoa cream cake
Chocolate protein truffles
Raw chocolate chip cookies
Raw chewy brownie bites
Cashew frosting
Chocolate frosting

MIX OF
RAW & BAKED
RECIPES

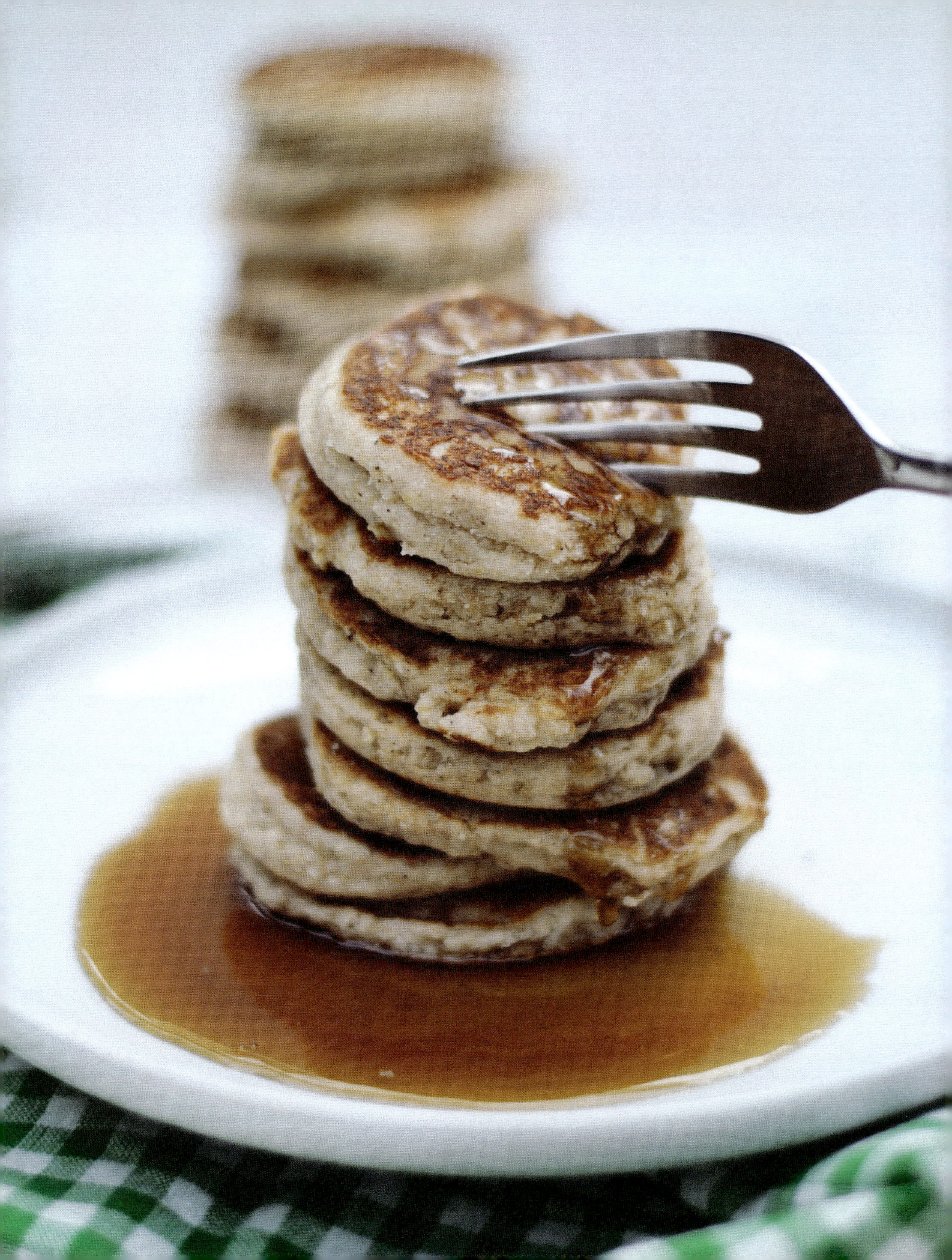

KEY BAKING INGREDIENTS

Our recipes have been tested and work the best with these key ingredients. But of course you can use anything you prefer. We do provide substitutions for each recipe. Our recipes are measured in ounces. If you prefer grams for weight measurements you can convert our recipes to grams.

Sorghum flour - A great basic flour that has neutral flavor and closely mimics regular flour. Brown rice is another good option.

Flax meal - Ground up flax seeds. Great for adding fiber to a recipe, but helps with texture and perfect egg substitute when you make as a flax gel.

Coconut flour - A high fiber, low in carb flour. A little goes a long way as it readily absorbs moisture. We feel in combination with sorghum and arrowroot all 3 together provide a nice soft light texture to the baked good. And as you will see we do not use eggs even though we use coconut flour; after many trials we found what we were looking for.

Coconut oil - Hands down our favorite oil to use in everything! In our recipes ALL coconut oil is measured in LIQUID form not solid! Lori has a great video on our YouTube channel (pure2rawtwins) showing how to melt it. Coconut oil provides a moist texture to the baked goods.

Coconut butter - A mix of coconut oil and coconut meat (comes from whole flesh coconut). A rich creamy "butter" that can be used in *most* recipes that call for coconut oil. We recommend having the butter softened when using in recipes, as it makes it easier to work with.

Raw cacao powder - We use (and recipes only tested with) RAW cacao powder, not processed cocoa powder that normally contains sugar. And of course raw cacao is full of antioxidants. **We have been using it for years for everything and love it, and have not used regular cocoa in a very long time.**

Arrowroot - Our favorite starch for lightness while providing a nice soft chew. It helps with the structure of the baked good, especially since our recipes do not have gums or eggs.

Coconut Sugar - A low glycemic sugar that looks like brown sugar. It is not as sweet as regular sugar, and provides a soft crumb texture instead of a crispy texture like other sugars.

Homemade buttermilk - You can use store bought, but we love to make a quick version at home when we need it. We use canned coconut milk (get organic if you can and FULL fat) and add 2-3 tablespoons of apple cider vinegar for 2 cups coconut milk. Let it sit for 10 minutes before using in recipes.

We do not use any gums in our recipes like you see in many gluten free products and recipes. Why we do not use xanthan or guar gum in our recipes is because of digestion. They can be rough on the stomach. But if you can handle them feel free to use them in our recipes, just remember a little goes a long way. No more than 1/2 tsp would be needed per recipe.

Other notes to remember when it comes to baking: different ovens can range in temperature and altitude can alter a recipe too.

We have played around with many different gluten-free flours (gf). The two gluten-free flours that we recommend starting your gf baking journey with are brown rice or sorghum flour. Once you get the feel of baking gf you can play around with other flours. We love the addition of mixing in coconut flour in our blend as it provides such a unique moistness to the baked goods. Our favorite starch is arrowroot, but you could use any other starch. If you want to use potato starch just remember it weighs heavier than other starches but does provide a lightness to each recipe. Have fun and play around with different flours to find what you like best. This is our go-to blend when we use gf blends in recipes.

We like a mix of gluten-free flours.

PURELY TWINS GF FLOUR BLEND

HOW WE MAKE OUR GLUTEN-FREE FLOUR BLEND.

Note: this blend is for our baked recipes not our raw recipes!

How we scoop our flours when measuring for a recipe: Lightly spoon flour into your measuring cup so that it is mounded and brimming over with flour. Then level off the extra flour with a knife .

What's wrong with scooping flour directly out of a flour bag or storage container? When you scoop flours and starches out of the bag the dry ingredients easily compact, causing you to add more flour, by volume, than a recipe actually calls for.

We also like to weigh out our ingredients in ounces that way we when remake a recipe we have a better guarantee it is going to come out! We highly recommend investing in a scale, you can purchase them at any retail kitchen stores.

Don't be afraid of trying new things and new blends. Each flour and starch provides something different to recipes. In this cookbook this is the blend we used in our recipes and had amazing results! So keep that in mind when you try the recipes with a different blend, it may or may not come out exactly like ours.

Ingredients:
1 cup brown rice flour or sorghum flour (4 1/2oz)
2/3 cup coconut flour (3oz)
2/3 cup arrowroot starch (2 1/2oz)

TIPS AND SUBSTITUTIONS

We suggest sorghum or brown rice flour to start baking gf because we feel those flours are the most similar to regular flour.

With our gf flour blend you could use some amaranth, quinoa or buckwheat flour replace the brown rice/sorghum - just remember it might alter the final taste and outcome.

Gf flours are all different in their own way, don't be afraid to try something different. Think outside the box!

Play around with different ratios but a good base is 2:1 *(2 cups flour to 1 cup starch).*

If you do not want to use gluten-free flours we suggest spelt flour.

Also our baked recipes have not been tested with store bought almond meal so we are unsure of how they would turn out.

We love freshly baked goods!

PURELY BAKED

We get excited planning out a recipe, making dirty dishes, taste testing along the way, and jumping up and down when we have a success. We feel like little scientists in the kitchen. Gluten-free vegan baking can be a little tricky, but we feel these recipes are perfected using our gluten-free all purpose flour blend. Please note these recipes work best using the ingredients we listed.

We hope you will add these recipes to your ever growing recipe collection.

We are here to share the love of baking...of food...of making new memories; maybe there will be some dancing in the kitchen with your loved ones. These baked recipes are some of our favorites. We hope they put a smile on your face.

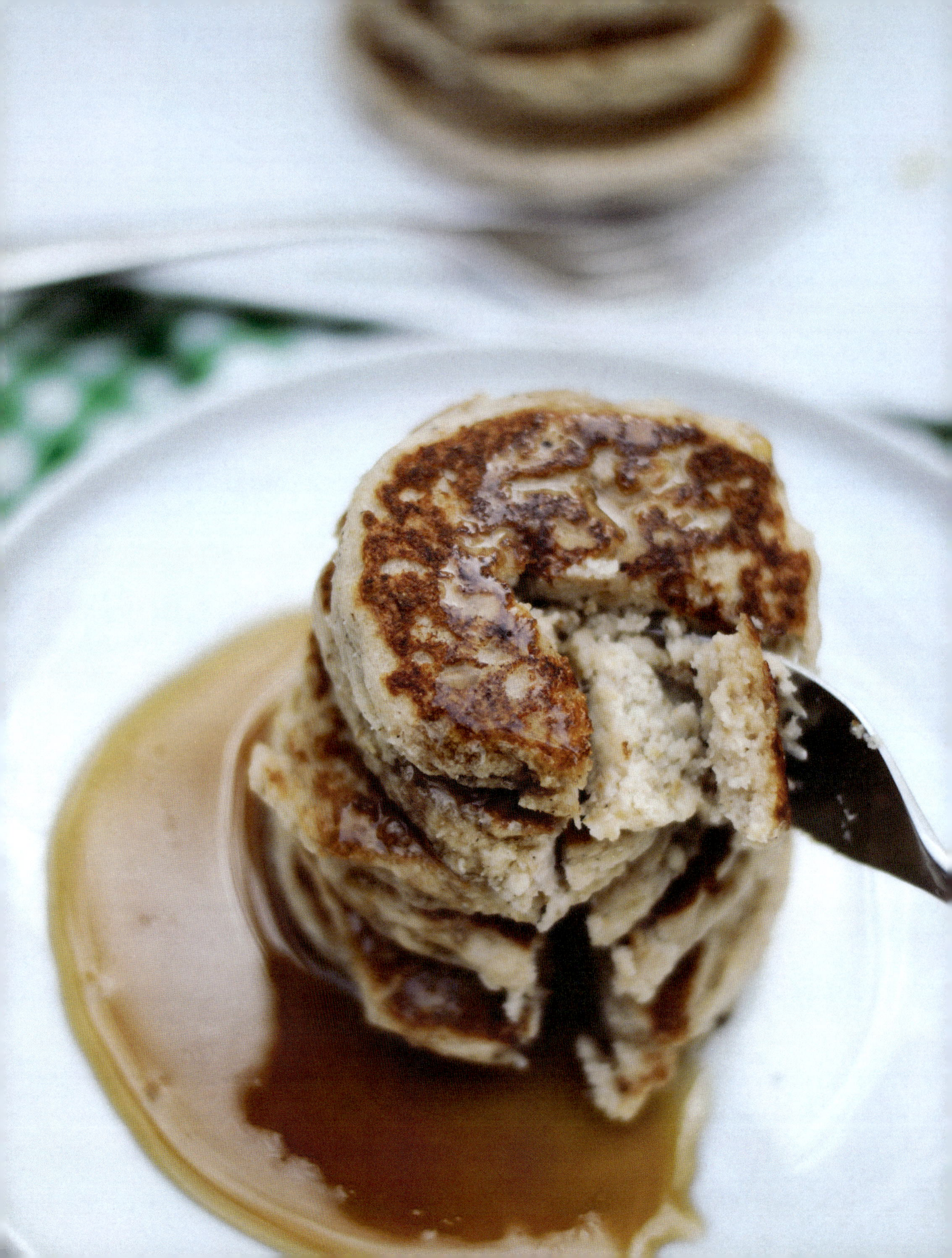

Michelle loves waking up before everyone else to whip up some pancakes for the family to enjoy. If there are any pancakes left, which usually they are none, she will happily finish them off. Due to not having any eggs, these pancakes tend to be moist and tender. These pancakes are great topped with some maple syrup.

Best way to start the day!

BUTTERMILK PANCAKES

Ingredients:
1 cup purelytwins gf blend (4oz)
2 tablespoons flax meal (1/2oz)
2 teaspoons baking powder
1/2 teaspoon baking soda
10 drops liquid stevia
2 tablespoons coconut oil, liquid (1oz)
2 tablespoons applesauce (1oz)
1 cup buttermilk (8oz)
2 teaspoons vanilla extract, optional

MAKES 12-14 PANCAKES USING (1 1/2 TBSP SCOOPER)

If making your own buttermilk, pour 1 can coconut milk or any other milk of choice (about 1 3/4 cups) with 2 tbsp apple cider vinegar in a glass cup. Let sit for 10 minutes.

In a large bowl place all dry ingredients. Whisk together. In another small bowl, place the wet ingredients except the buttermilk. And stir. Next add wet ingredients into dry ingredient bowl. Whisk ingredients together. Start to pour in buttermilk. Continue to whisk. Batter will be on the thick runny side.

Using a pre-heated skillet over medium heat, begin to scoop pancake batter onto skillet. Cook a few minutes on each side, until golden brown.

Top pancakes with maple syrup and/or your favorite toppings.

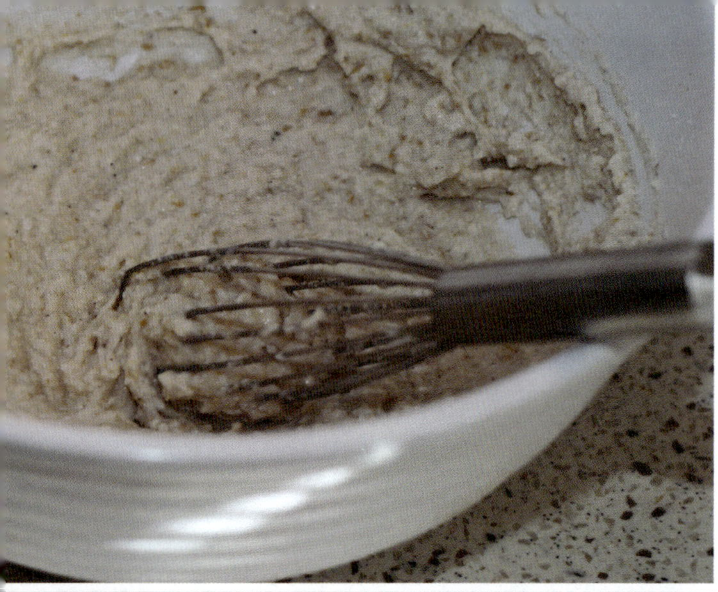
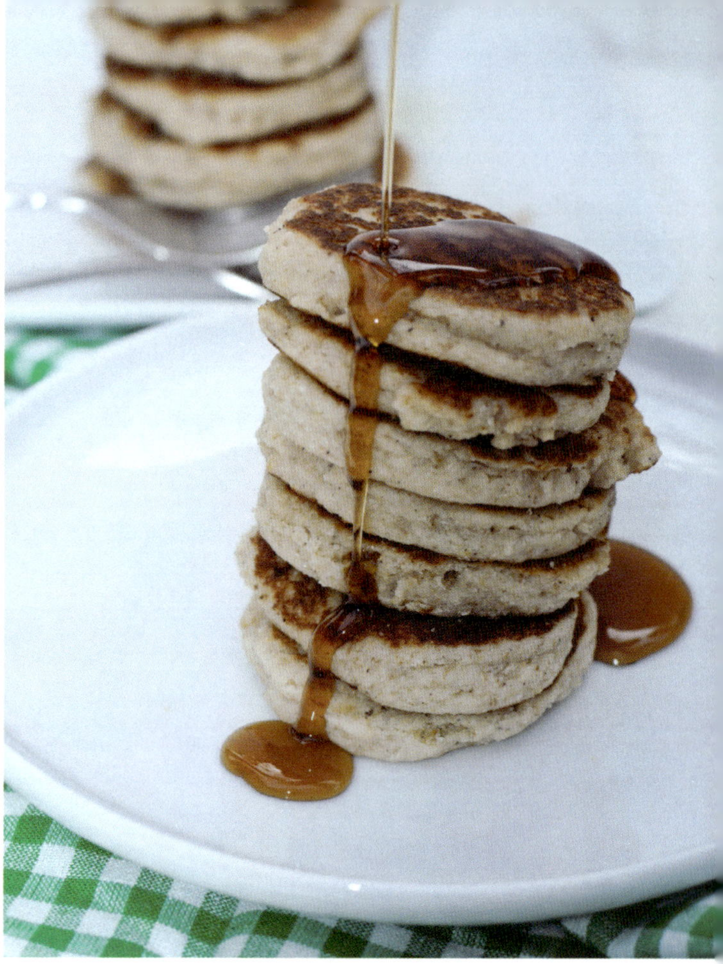
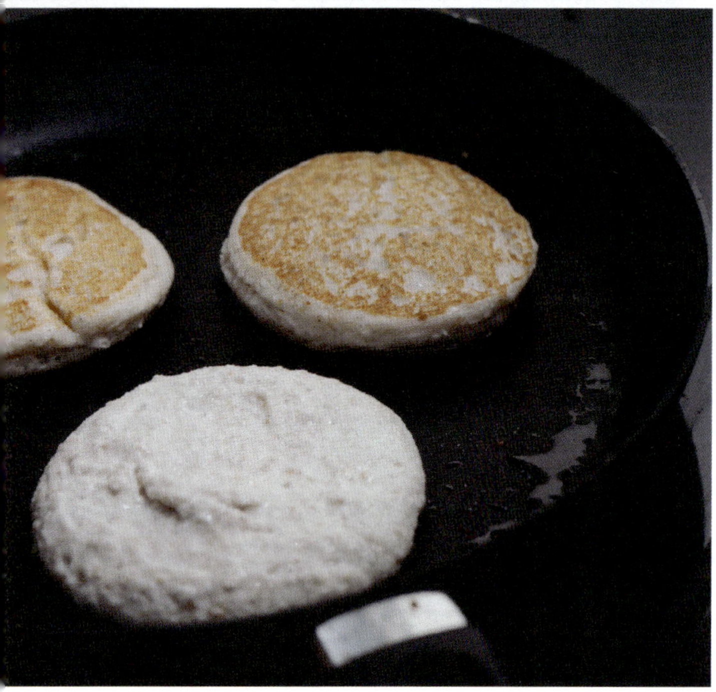
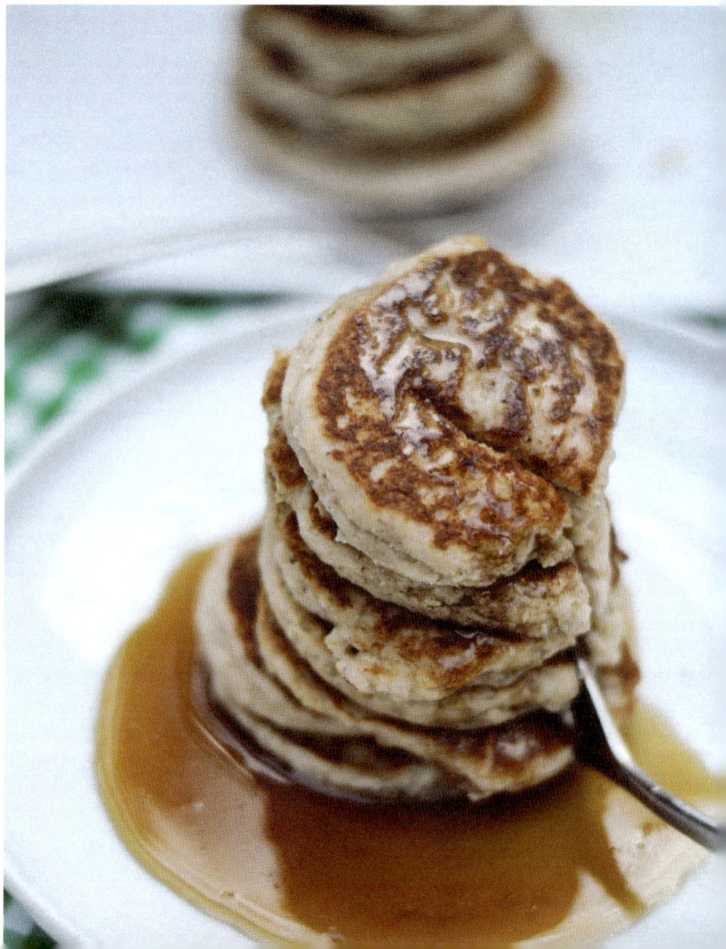
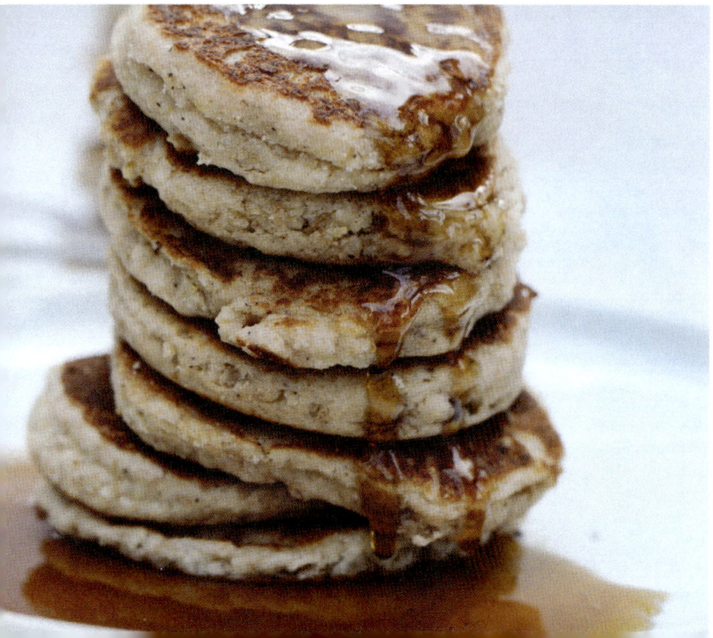

TIPS AND SUBSTITUTIONS

Make sure all ingredients are at room temperature. If things are a little chilly, we suggest heating up buttermilk some before pouring into batter. This will help make it easier to work with.
You may use any gluten-free or flour blend of your choice instead of our gf blend.
May use 2 tbsp more flour or chia seeds to replace flax meal.
You may use almond or soy milk to replace coconut milk, or pre-made buttermilk.
If you do not have liquid steiva, you could omit or add 1 tbsp of sugar.
To replace applesauce, you could use sweet potato or pumpkin puree, or 1 egg.

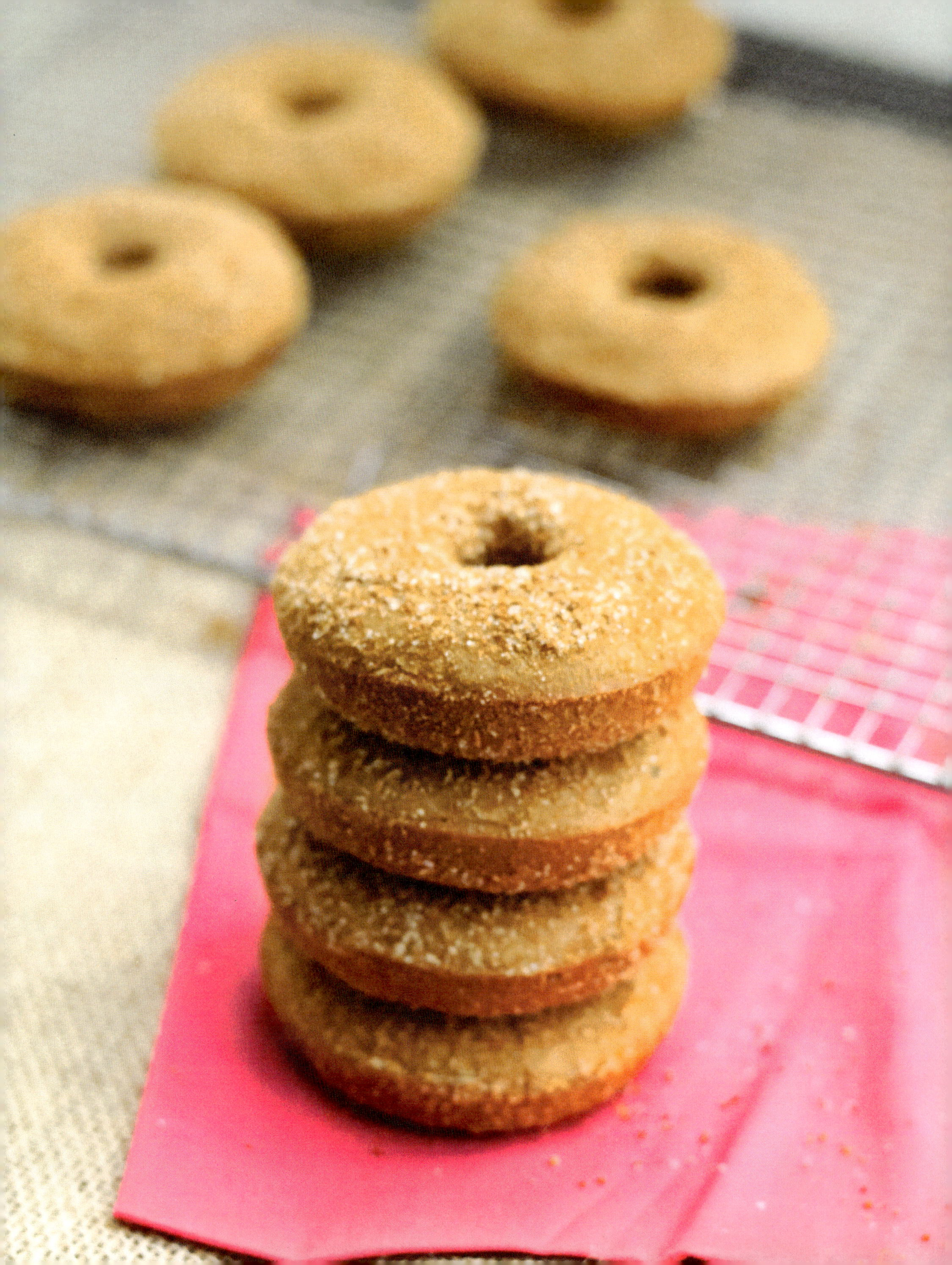

Who doesn't love a sweet cake-like donut? We sure do! We love baked donuts because they are easy to make and better for you. This is a basic donut recipe that is light, with a slight spongy chew to them. You can coat this donut with any toppings from cinnamon sugar, melted chocolate to our cashew frosting.

Perfect to enjoy with a cup of coffee or tea.

BASIC BAKED DONUTS

Ingredients:
1 cup purelytwins gf blend + 2 tablespoons (4 1/2oz)
2 1/2 teaspoons baking powder
1 teaspoon vanilla extract
1/8 teaspoon ground nutmeg
1/2 cup coconut sugar (3oz)
3 tablespoons coconut oil, liquid (1 1/2oz)
2 tablespoons coconut butter, softened (1 1/4oz)
1 cup buttermilk (8oz)

Cinnamon sugar mixture:
2/3 cup sugar
1 tablespoon +1 teaspoon ground cinnamon
about 1 tablespoon coconut oil, liquid

makes 6 donuts

If you do not have buttermilk, you can make your own by taking 1 can of coconut milk (about 1 3/4 cups) or any milk of choice and add 2 tablespoons apple cider vinegar. Let sit for 10 minutes.

In a large bowl place all dry ingredients. Whisk together. Next cut in coconut butter and coconut oil. Cut until you achieve pea-like batter. Then pour in buttermilk. Stir until batter comes together. Should be a nice smooth batter. Pipe or spoon batter into lightly greased donut pan. Place in 350 degree oven. Bake for about 13-15 minutes until toothpick comes out clean, and firm to the touch. Once out of oven let cool for a little bit then remove from pan.

To coat with cinnamon sugar: lightly coat each donut with coconut oil (in liquid form) and toss with cinnamon sugar mixture.

Donuts are best eaten the same day they are made.

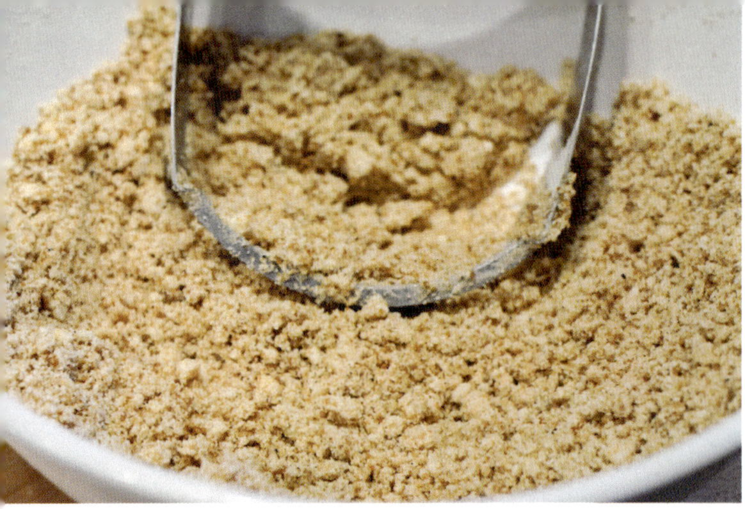
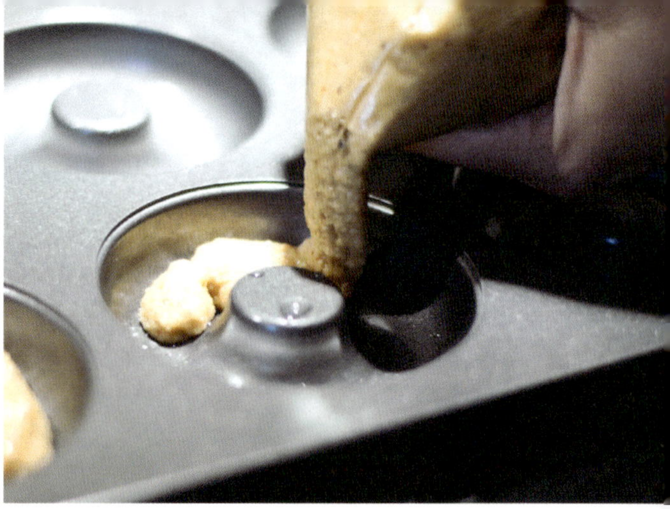
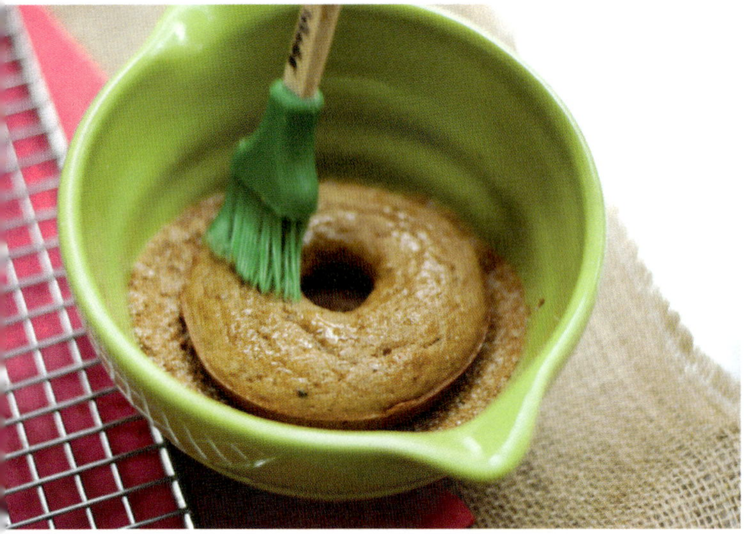
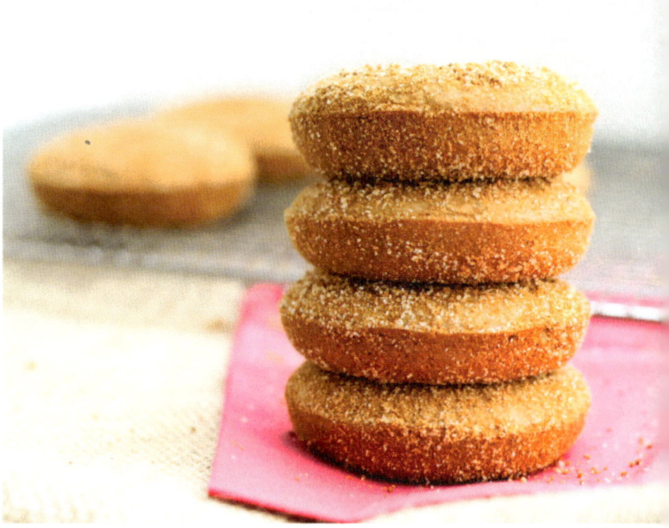
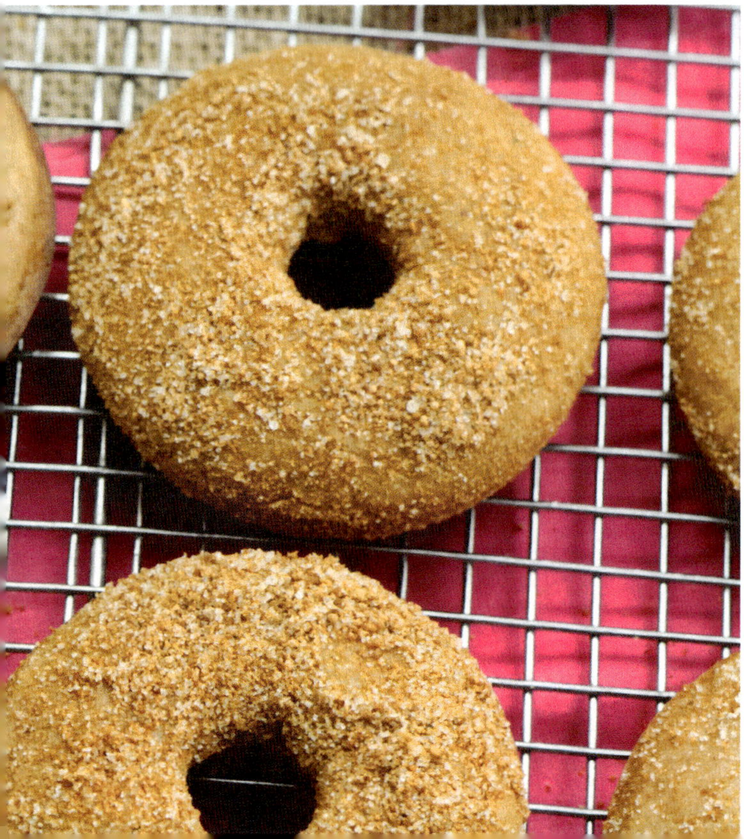
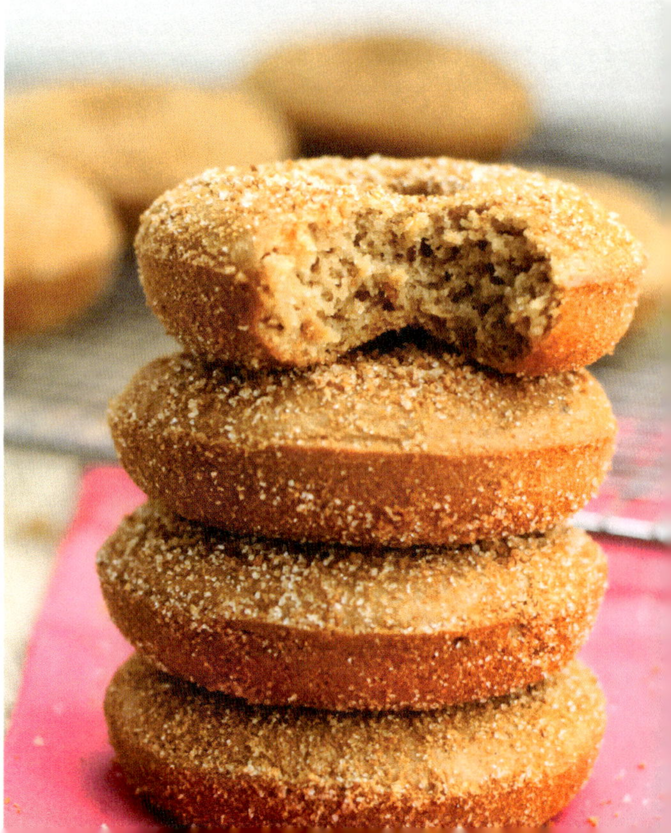

TIPS AND SUBSTITUTIONS

You may use any gluten-free or flour blend of your choice instead of our gf blend.
You could do all coconut oil and no coconut butter, we just like using a mix of the two as we feel it provides a nice texture to the donuts.
You could use soy butter or a high quality grass-fed butter instead of coconut butter.
With the sugars, you could use coconut sugar or regular sugar.
We have not tried this recipe with a liquid sweetener nor stevia so we are unsure of how it would come out.
For the 2 tablespoons of more gf blend you use potato starch as we find that helps provide a very nice light texture.
If you would like to add an egg, reduce the buttermilk down to 3/4 cup.
If you do not have a donut pan, can bake them in muffin pan (filled half way) and cooking time may vary.

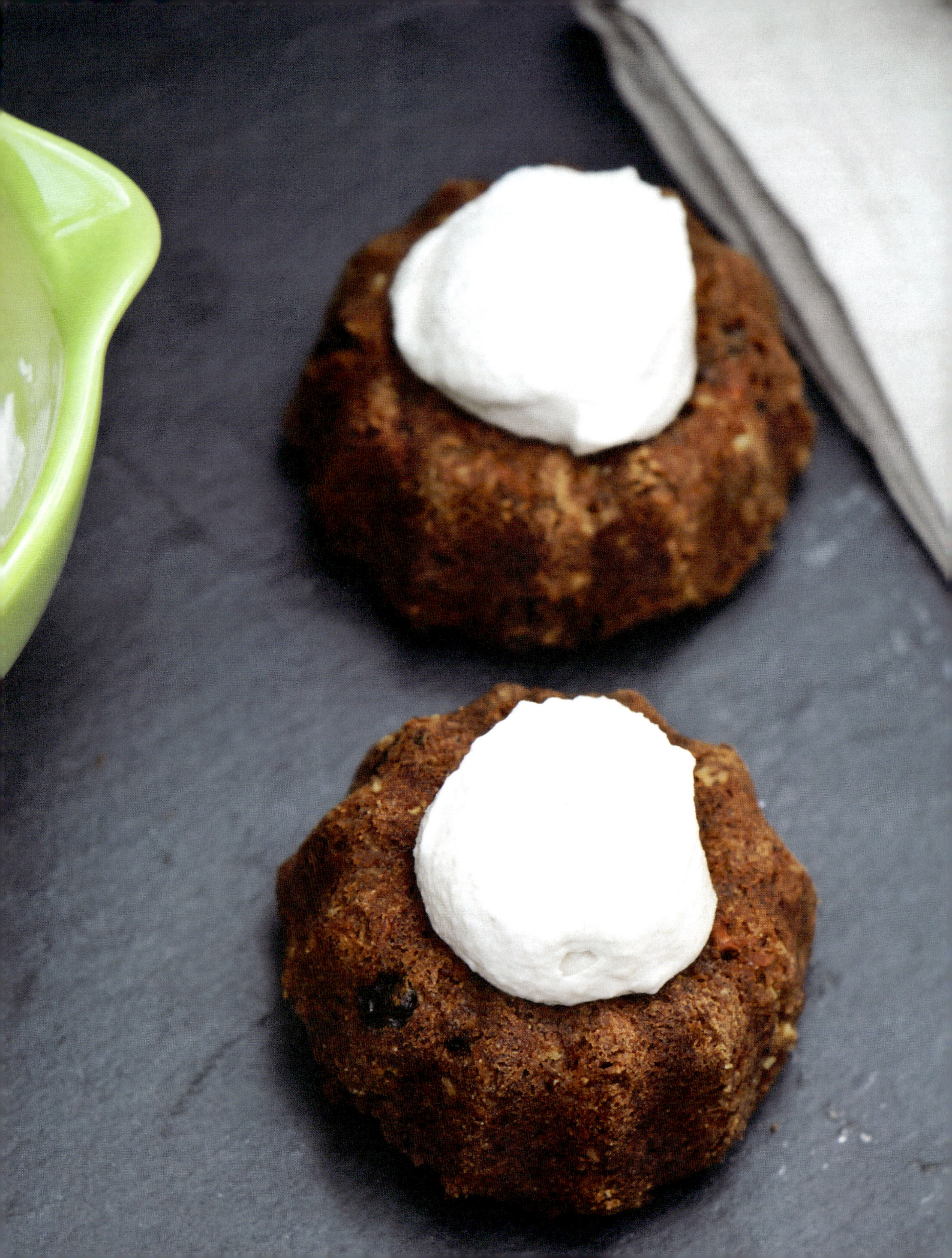

A top favorite of ours! Every mouthful is filled with creaminess from the cashew frosting and spice from the cake. We use no nuts or pineapple, as we prefer the wonderful texture the raisins and coconut flakes provide our cakes. This is our go-to carrot cake recipe. Moist. Dense. Flavorful. Everything you would want in a little and more cake!

Perfect blend of spice & sweetness.

INDIVIDUAL CARROT CAKES

Ingredients:
- 1 1/2 cups purelytwins blend (6oz)
- 1 tablespoon baking powder
- 1 teaspoon baking soda
- 2 teaspoons cinnamon
- 1/2 teaspoon nutmeg
- 1/4 teaspoon cloves
- 1/4 teaspoon cardamom
- 3 tablespoons flax meal (3/4oz)
- 6 tablespoons water (to make egg gel)
- 2 teaspoons vanilla extract
- 2 large carrots shredded (5oz)
- 1/2 cup raisins
- 1/3 cup coconut flakes (1oz)
- 1/2 cup applesauce (4oz)
- 6 tablespoons coconut oil, liquid (3oz)
- 1 cup coconut sugar (6 oz)
- 1/2 cup warm water

makes 8-9 mini cakes

First make flax gel. Take 3 tbsp flax meal with 6 tbsp water in a bowl and let sit for at least 10 minutes. Looking for a thick gel-like texture.

In a large bowl place dry ingredients (flour, spices, and sugar). Whisk together. When flax gel is ready add it to dry ingredients, along with vanilla, shredded carrots, raisins, coconut flakes, applesauce and coconut oil. Stir together. End with adding the warm water. This helps keep coconut oil liquid making it easier to stir.

Place in 6 mini bundt cake (or large muffin pan) baking pan, lightly greased. Place in 325 degree oven and bake for 25-30 minutes, or until toothpick comes out clean. Top with our cashew frosting.

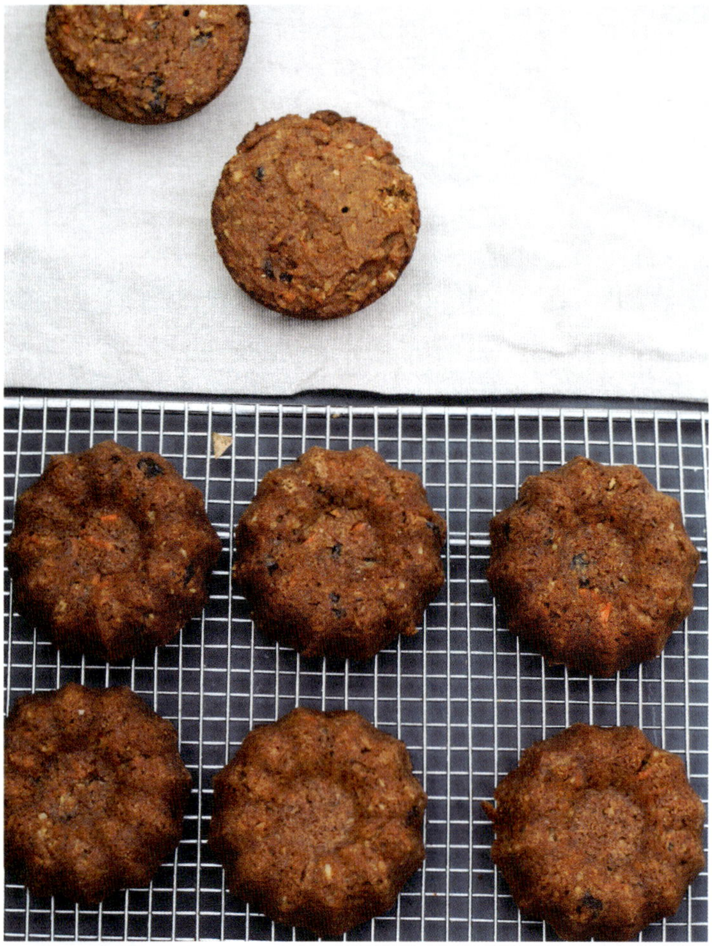
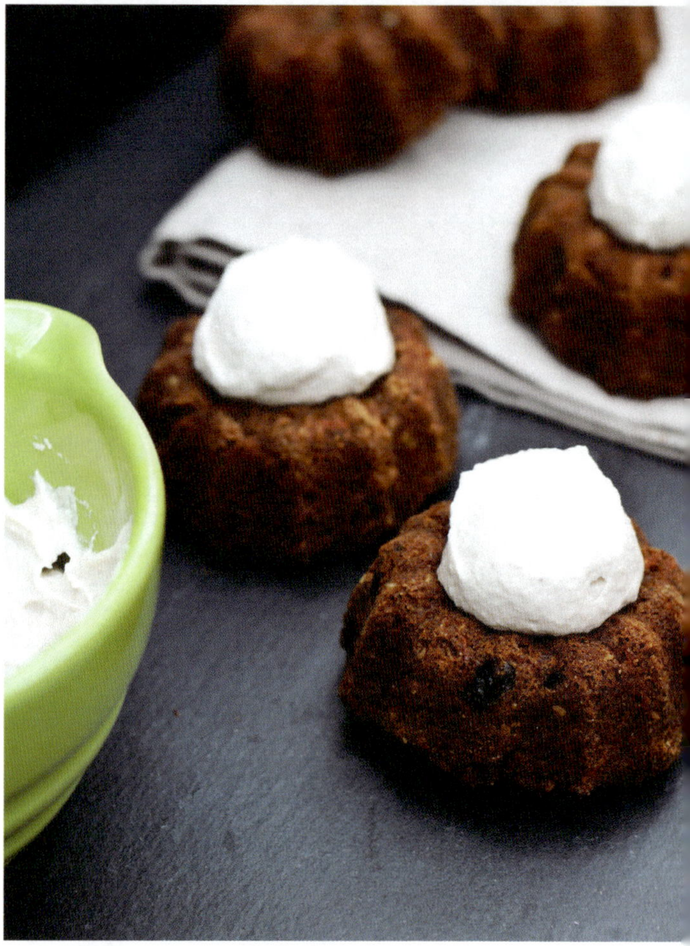
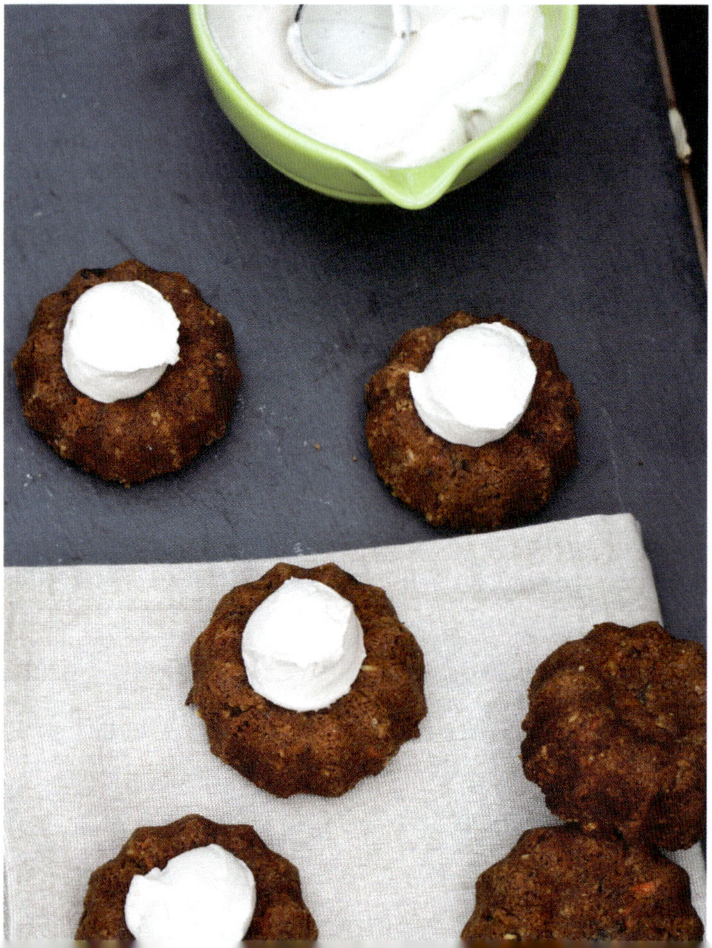
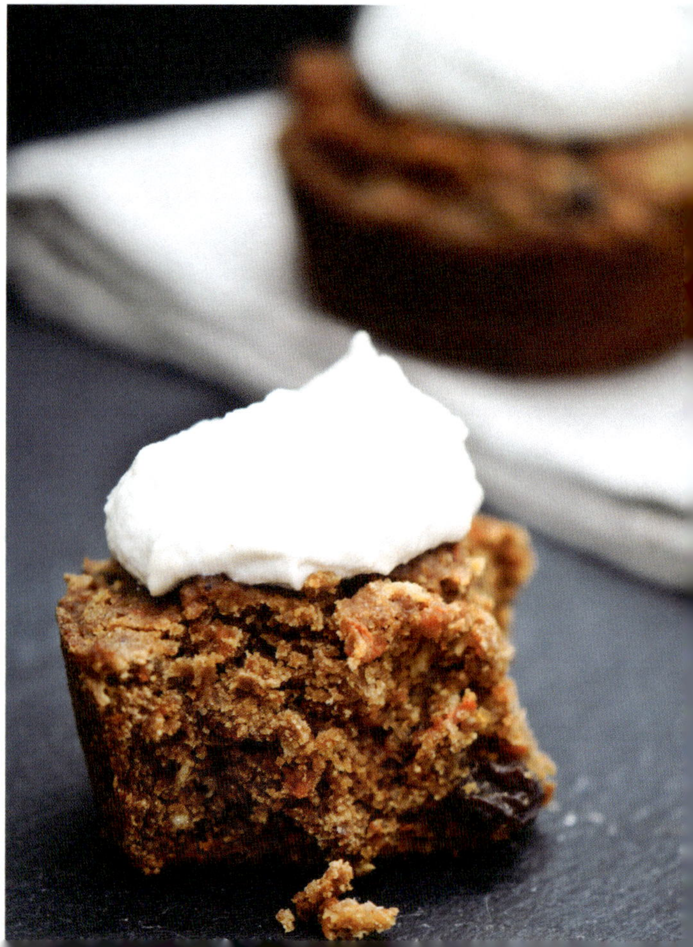

TIPS AND SUBSTITUTIONS

You may use any gluten-free or flour blend of your choice instead of our gf blend.
If you would like to use a liquid sweetener instead of coconut sugar, you will have to reduce the water. You might not even need water. Start small adding 1 tbsp at a time as you want a thick batter.
You could also use 2 eggs instead of flax gel if you want. If you do use eggs you might need to reduce water, so slowy add it in.
Sweet potato puree can be used instead of applesauce.
Grapeseed oil can be used instead of coconut oil.
If you like nuts in your carrot cake, please feel free to add a handful of your favorite chopped nuts.

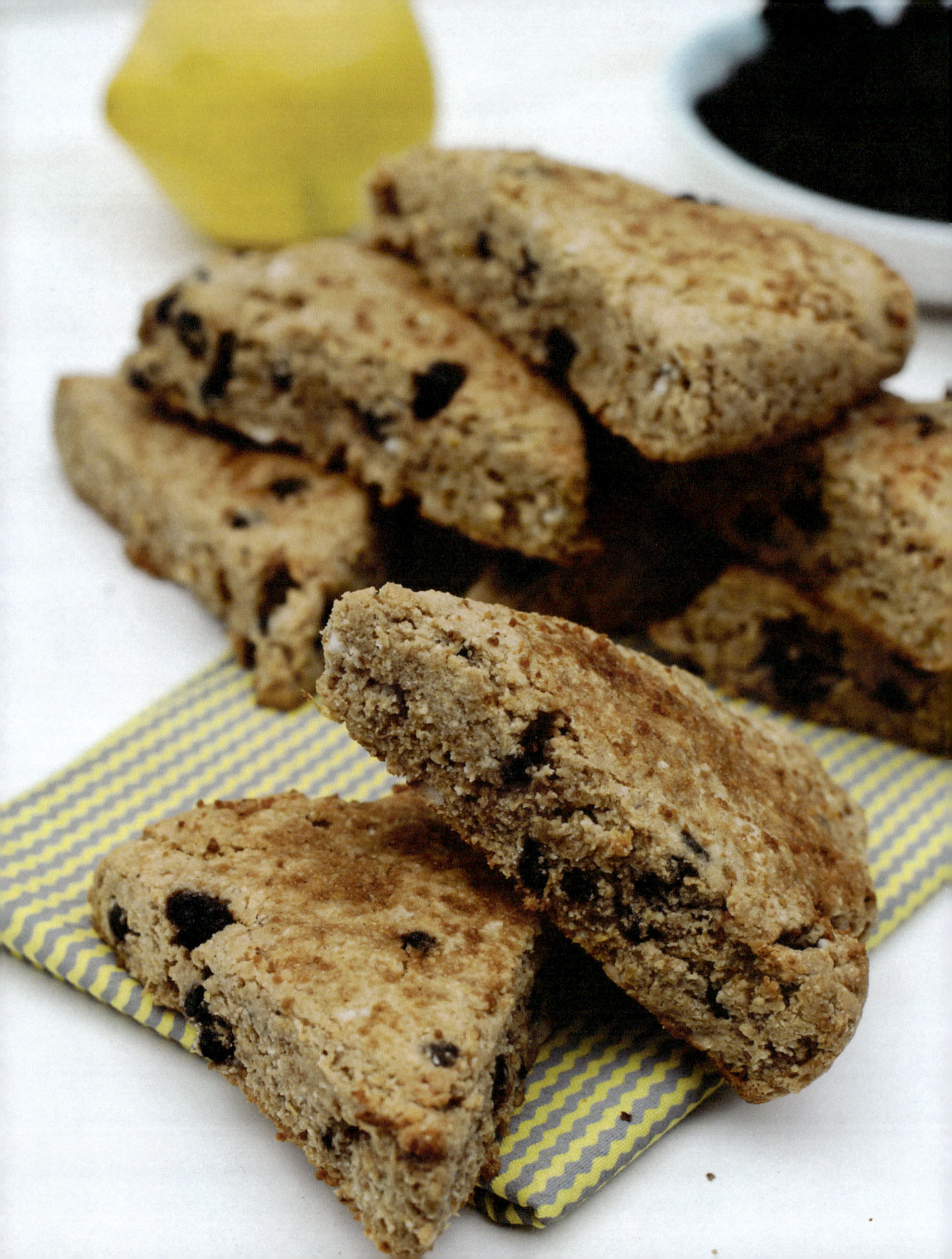

We were never scone lovers until we made these for the first time a little over 4 years ago. We were hooked! Plus, they are a super easy recipe to make and it's simple to create new flavors to devour. These scones are not your average scone; they are soft and moist with an abundance of flavor that is so satisfying.

Loved by everyone, even gluten lovers.

Lemon Blueberry Scones

Ingredients:
1 1/2 cups purelytwins gf blend (6oz)
2 1/4 teaspoons baking powder
1/2 cup coconut sugar (3oz)
3 tablespoons flax meal (3/4 oz)
6 tablespoons water
3 tablespoons coconut oil, liquid (1 1/2oz)
1/4 cup coconut butter, softened (2 1/2oz)
1 zest of a large lemon
2 tablespoons lemon juice
1/3 cup dry blueberries (2oz)
6-8 tablespoons buttermilk (3-4oz)

makes 8 scones

First make flax gel. Place 3 tbsp flax meal with 6 tbsp water in a bowl. Let sit for 10 mintues to form a thick gel.

In a large bowl place all dry ingredients. Whisk together. Next cut coconut oil and coconut butter into your dry ingredients. Cut until you get a pea-like batter. Add in flax gel, lemon zest and juice and dried blueberries. Continue to stir. Slowly add in buttermilk by tablespoon until you get an easy to work with batter.

Place scone batter on cookie tray and mold into a circle. Cut into wedges. Then pull apart wedges for more even baking.

Place in 375 degree oven. Bake for about 18-20 minutes until easy to pick up and a little golden on bottom.

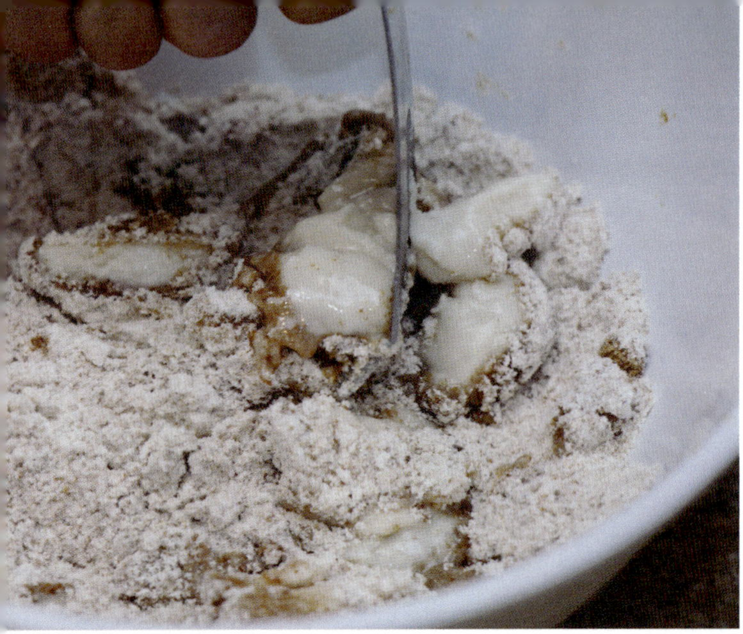
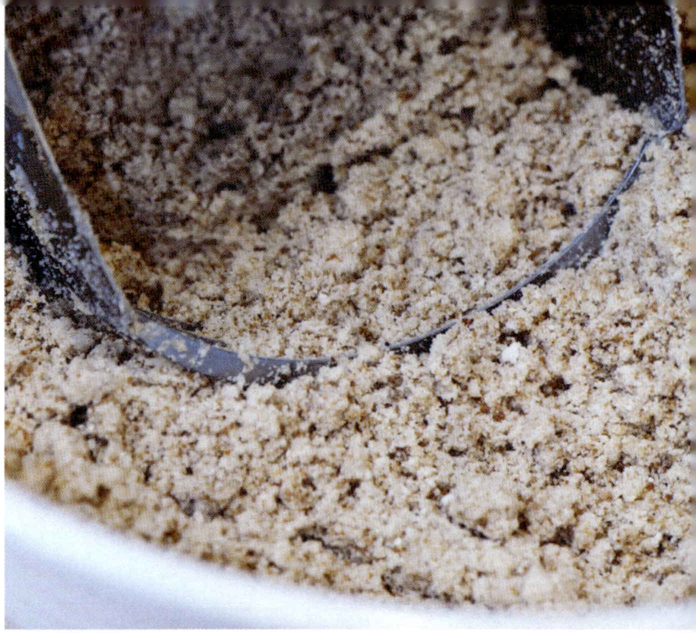
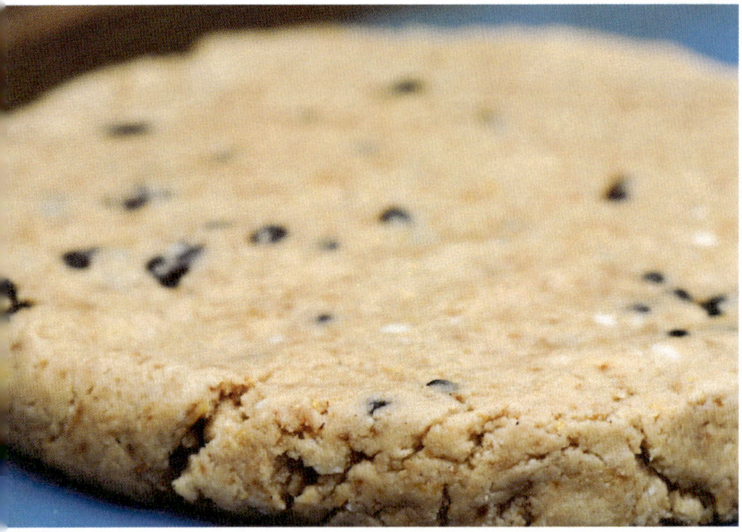
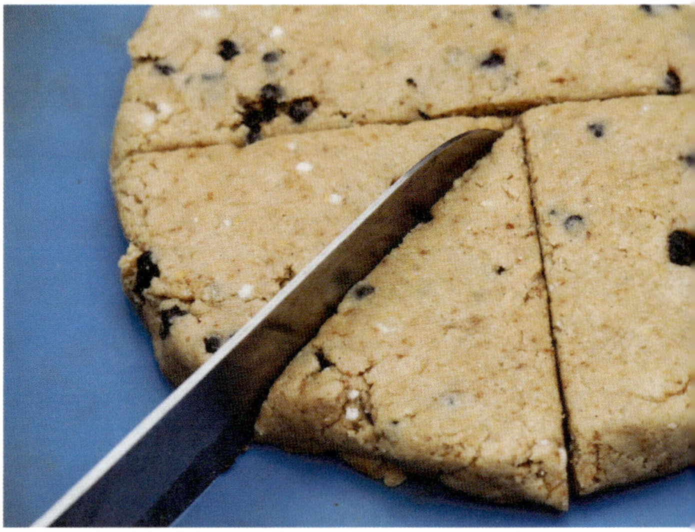
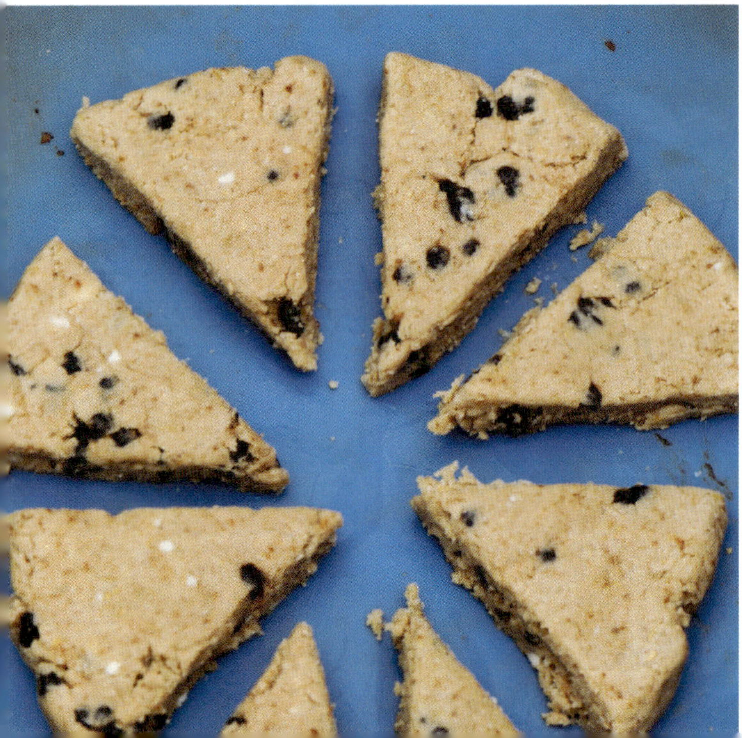
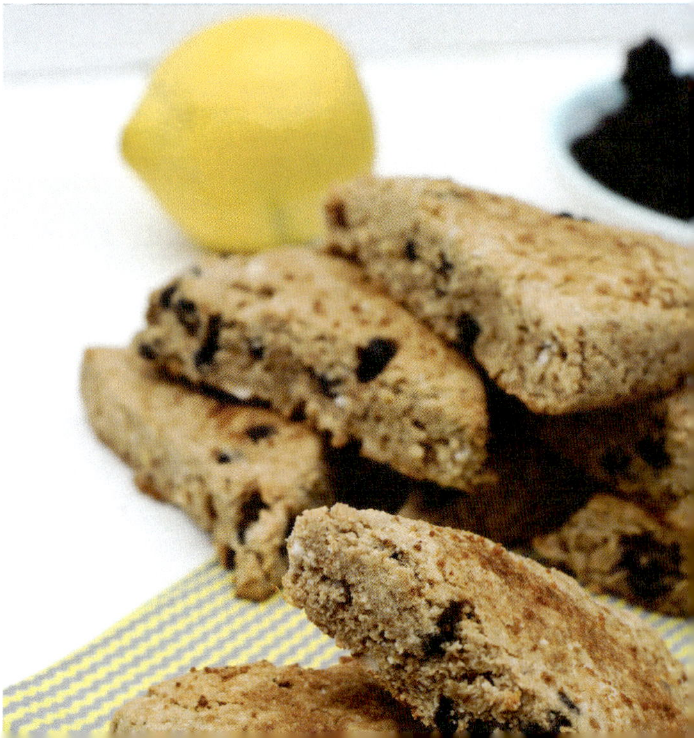

TIPS AND SUBSTITUTIONS

You may use any gluten-free or flour blend of your choice instead of our gf blend. You could use all coconut oil and omit coconut butter. We prefer using a mix of the two as we feel it provides a nice texture to the scones. **You will get a few little chunks of coconut butter in the scones.**

You could use soy butter or a high quality grass-fed butter instead of coconut butter. With the sugars, you could use coconut sugar or regular sugar. You can use a liquid sweetener, just reduce buttermilk by a few tablespoons. You want the batter to be moist, sticky, easy to work with, not runny.

We have found we get the best results with dried fruit over fresh fruit.

You can use 2 eggs to replace the flax gel if desired.

Before baking you can top each scone with a little more sugar for a little extra sweetness on top.

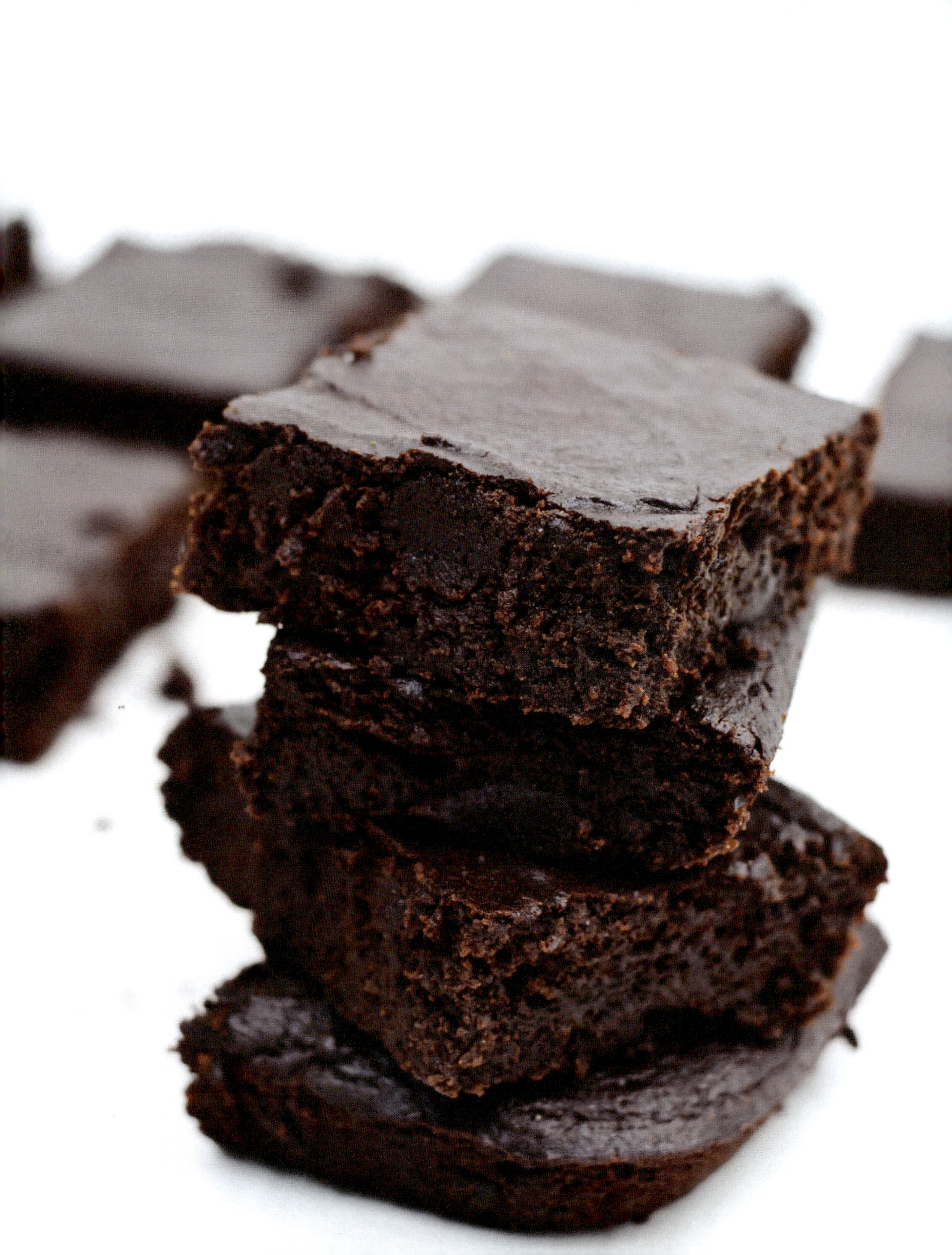

We love a good chocolate fudgy brownie. We make our brownies with cacao powder instead of melting chocolate and we still find these to be super rich dense moist brownies. Even non brownie lovers love this recipe! *These are also good cold!* This recipe is by far our favorite brownie recipe.

You have been warned.

FUDGY BROWNIES

Ingredients:
1 cup + 2 tablespoons purelytwins gf flour (4 1/2oz)
1 cup cacao powder (3 1/4oz)
2 tablespoons mesquite (1/2oz)
1/4 teaspoon baking soda
1 1/4 cups coconut sugar (6 1/4oz)
1/2 cup + 2 tablespoons coconut oil, liquid (5oz)
1/2 cup + 2 tablespoons sweet potato puree (5oz)
2 teaspoons vanilla extract
3/4 cup warm water

MAKES 12 BROWNIES

In a large bowl place all dry ingredients. Whisk together. In another small bowl, place all wet ingredients except the water. Stir together. Then add wet to dry ingredients bowl. And stir together. Start to slowly pour in your warm water. Continue to stir.

Pour brownie batter into 11x7 glass baking dish lightly greased with coconut oil.

Place in 325 degree oven. Bake for about 30-35 minutes. Until toothpick comes out mostly clean, all depends on how gooey you like your brownies.

Let cool completely before cutting. Enjoy at room temperature or cold from refrigerator.

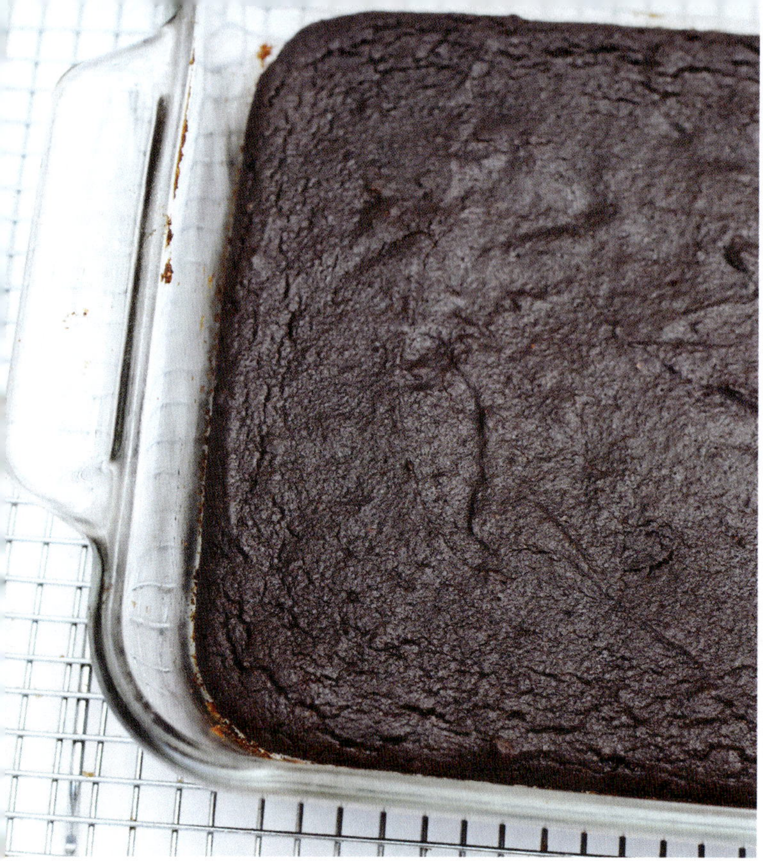
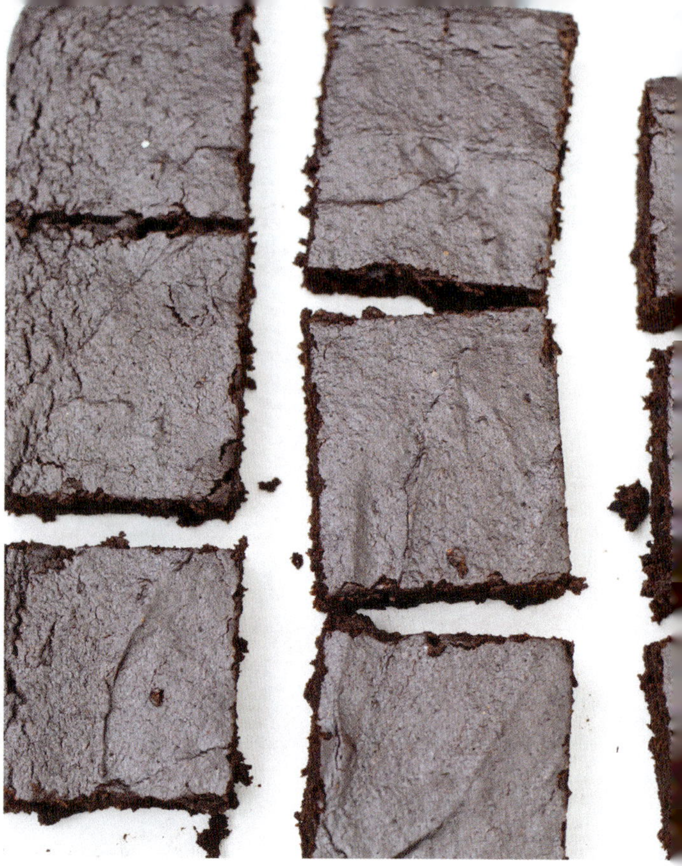
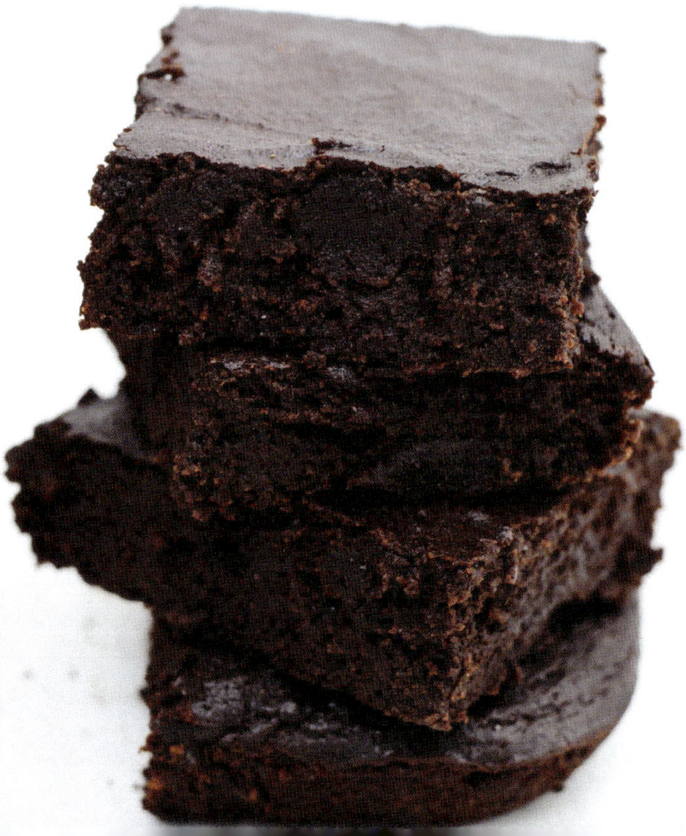
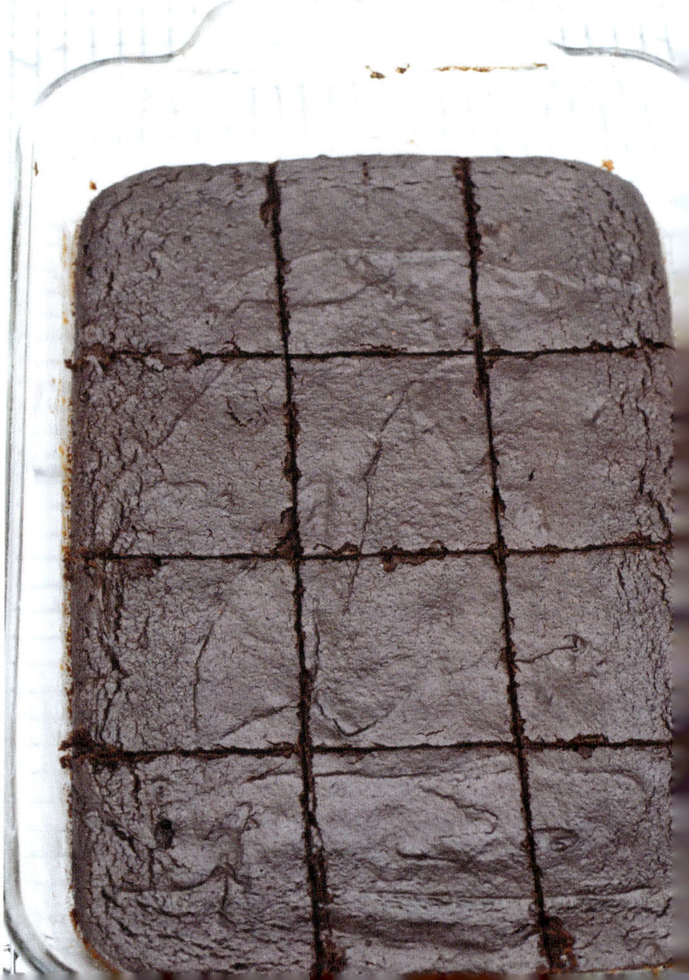

TIPS AND SUBSTITUTIONS

If you do not have mesquite you can use 2 tbsp sorghum flour or any other gluten-free flour.

You may use any gluten-free or flour blend of your choice instead of our gf blend.

If you prefer to use a liquid sweetener for the coconut sugar, we suggest reducing water by 3-4 tbsp and slowly add it in.

Pumpkin puree would be the best replacement for the sweet potato puree; we have not had good results with applesauce for this recipe.

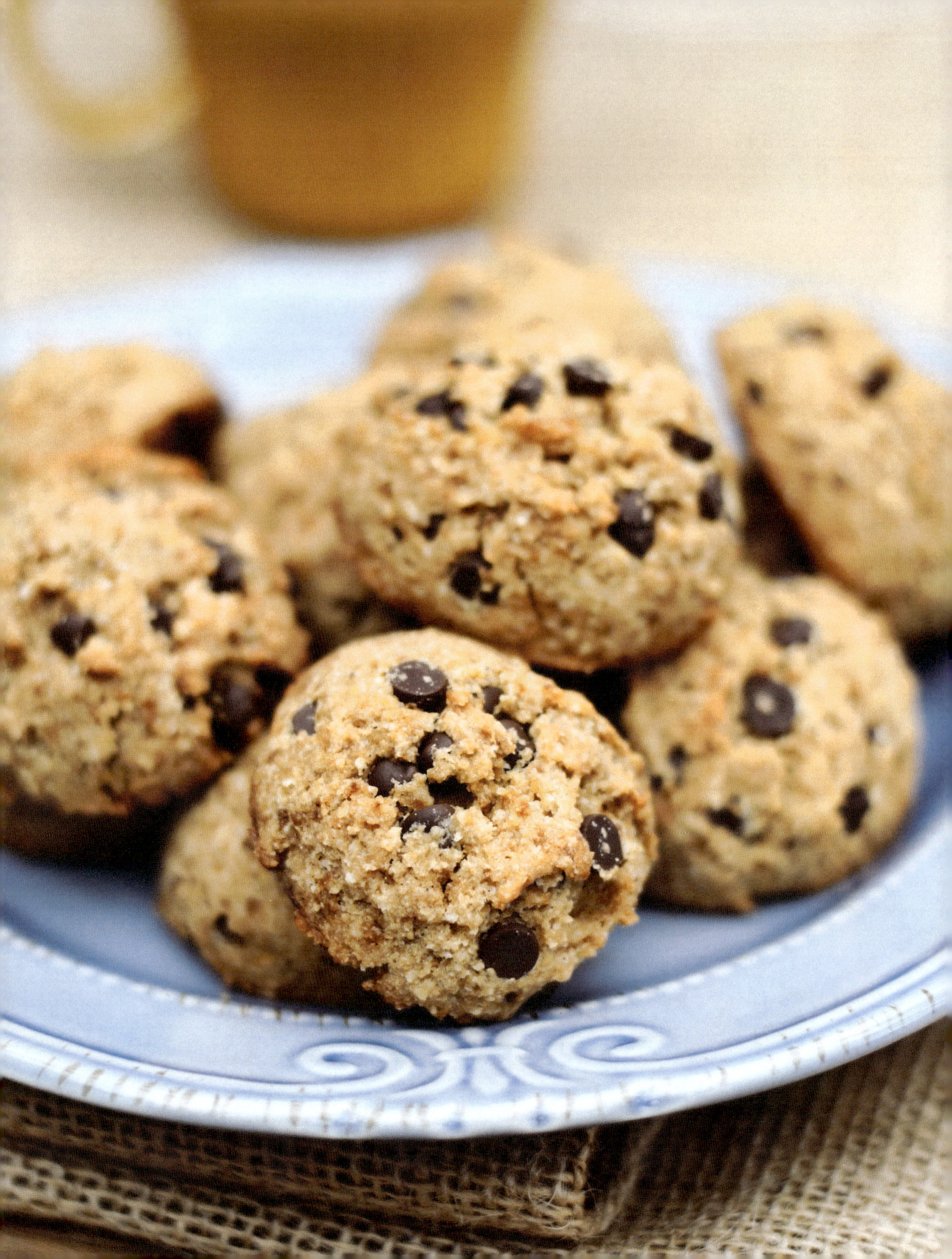

There are so many varieties of chocolate chip cookies out there...thin, cripsy, cake-like...is there a perfect cookie? We feel our recipe is pretty darn close! Chocolate chip cookies are our top favorite dessert to make over and over, which we do! This recipe is easy to make and creates a soft, melt-in-your-mouth chocolate chip cookie.

Who wants some cookies?

CHOCOLATE CHIP COOKIES

Ingredients:
2 cups purelytwins GF blend (8oz)
1/2 teaspoon baking soda
3/4 cup coconut sugar (4 oz)
1/4 cup maple syrup (2 3/4oz)
1/2 cup coconut oil, liquid (4oz)
2 teaspoons vanilla extract
3 tablespoons flax meal
6 tablespoons water
2/3 cup chocolate chips (5oz)

MAKES ABOUT 33 COOKIES USING 1 1/2 TBSP SCOOPER

First make flax gel. Place 3 tbsp flax meal with 6 tbsp water in a bowl. Let sit for 10 minutes to form a thick gel.

In a large bowl place all dry ingredients. Whisk together. Add in chocolate chips and stir to combine. Next add flax gel, coconut oil, maple syrup, and vanilla into your dry ingredient bowl. Mix together. Scoop cookies using a cookie scooper or spoon onto a parchment lined cookie tray. May leave round, or press down to flatten.

Place in 325 degree oven. Bake for about 18-20 minutes. Let cool before removing from tray as they are delicate when hot due to coconut oil being sensitive to heat.

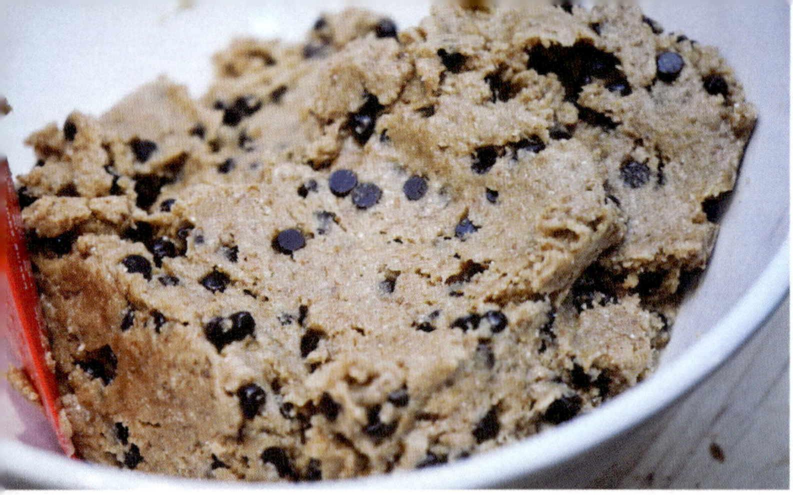
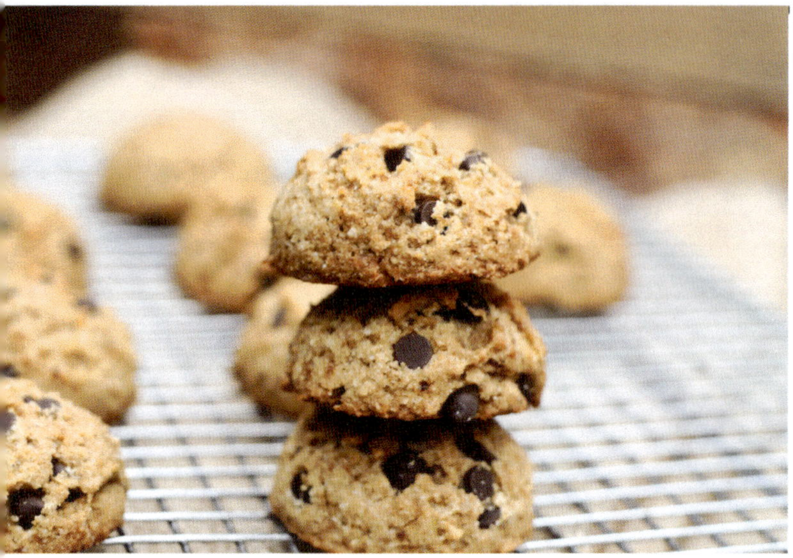
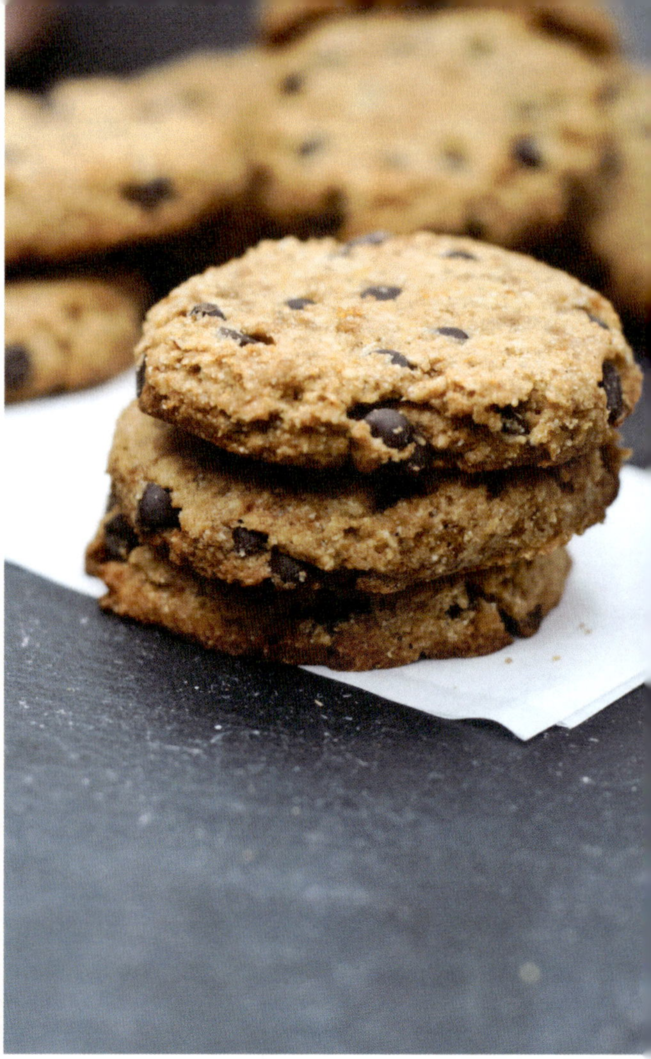
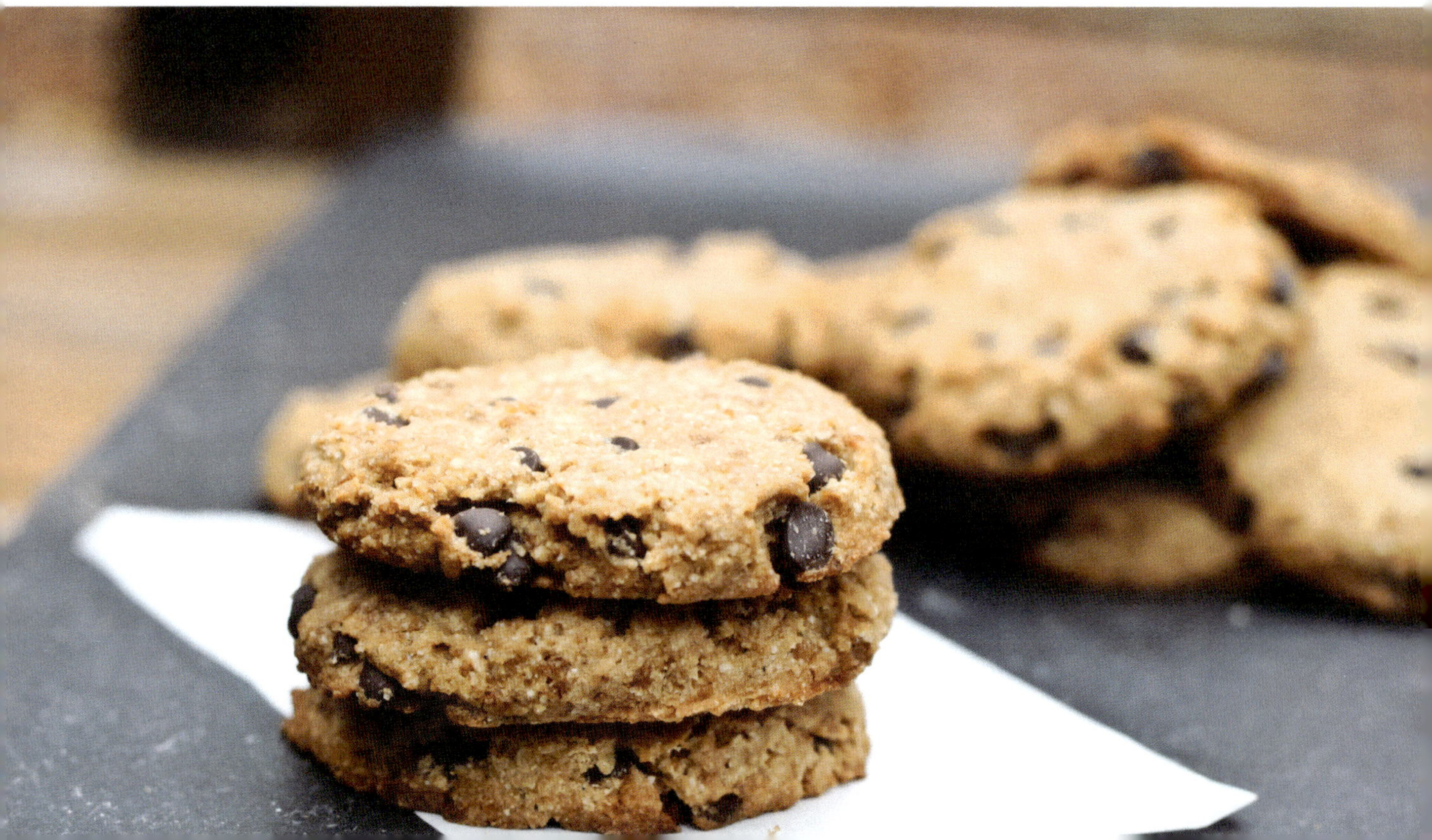

TIPS AND SUBSTITUTIONS

You may use any gluten-free or flour blend of your choice instead of our gf blend.

To replace flax gel you can use 2 eggs.

You could use melted butter of choice for the coconut oil.

Depending on what sugar you use in this recipe, might alter the final flavor and texture. We find coconut sugar provides a softer cookie; whereas regular sugar provides more sweetness and a crisper cookie.

Honey, agave, or coconut nectar can replace the maple syrup.

KEY RAW INGREDIENTS

Our recipes have been tested and work the best with these key ingredients. But of course you can use anything you prefer. We do provide substitutions for each recipe. Our recipes are measured in ounces. If you prefer grams for weight measurements you can convert our recipes to grams.

Mesquite - A pod that comes from the mesquite tree. Has a distinct flavor, a little sweet with a carmel smokey flavor (similar to carob powder).

Lucuma - Sold in powdered form that comes from a fruit. Used most often in ice creams. A has natural sweet flavor, but very unique at the same time.

Coconut oil - Hands down our favorite oil to use in everything! In our recipes ALL coconut oil is measured in LIQUID form not solid! Lori has a great video on our YouTube channel (pure2rawtwins) showing how to melt it. **Coconut oil has NO real substitute as it provides the hard body texture that holds the raw desserts together.**

Coconut butter - A mix of coconut oil and coconut meat (comes from whole flesh coconut). A rich creamy "butter" that can be used in *most* recipes that call for coconut oil. We recommend having the butter softened when using in recipes, as it makes it easier to work with.

Raw cacao powder - We use (and recipes only tested with) RAW cacao powder, not processed cocoa powder that normally contains sugar. And of course raw cacao is full of antioxidants. **We have been using it for years for everything and love it, and have not used regular cocoa in a very long time.**

Cacao butter - A pale yellow edible vegetable fat extracted from the cacao bean. It is used in making chocolate bars. It is a solid fat that does not melt like coconut oil.

Coconut nectar - A low glycemic liquid sweetener. It is not as sweet as regular sugar, and provides a softer and chewier result than using maple syrup. Very sticky to work with like honey.

Our recipes are based off using raw nuts and seeds, so if you use roasted please note it will change the final flavor.

Notes about dehydrating your foods. Dehydrating is a low temperture method of "baking" that removes the water resulting in a dry crispy product. Those of you who would love to keep recipes RAW and do not have a dehydrator, we recommend experimenting with your oven. We feel using a dehydrator does a better job. You cannot make too many mistakes with raw foods, like you can in baking. Raw foods are fun, easy, and nutritous.

Go wild in the kitchen!

Making date paste is really easy. There really is no wrong or right way to make date paste. Everyone has their own technique for making it. You could use any date paste of your liking in our recipes that call for it. But we wanted to share how we make ours. We like our date paste thick and a little chunky; please adjust to your preference. You may also add in some vanilla or pinch of sea salt if desired.

We adore medjool dates.

DATE PASTE

Ingredients:
12-14 medjool dates, pitted
5 tablespoons water

MAKES ABOUT 3/4 CUP DATE PASTE

Paste will last about 5-7 days in refrigerator.

Take the pit out of your medjool dates. To make it easier to blend in Vita-mix or blender, we recommend soaking the pitted dates for a few minutes. Then remove from water (save this water to use in making paste) and place soaked dates into blender.
Begin to blend. Slowly start adding water until you get a thick paste texture. You can add in more water if you want your date paste more smooth and less thick.

We make our nut flours, as we like to call them, different from most. You typically see people using leftover nut milk pulp that they dry out and use as their nut meal. We don't do that as we do not drink that much nut milks. We just soak our nuts for a few hours or overnight, rinse and dehydrate to dry the nuts out. Then we place the dry nuts in our food processor (Vita-mix would work) and grind into nut meal/flour.

Homemade raw nut flours.

PURELY TWINS NUT FLOURS

cashew flour - made from grinding up whole cashews in a food processor or high powered blender to get a fine meal, flour-like texture

almond and/or hazelnut flour - made from grinding up whole almonds or hazelnuts in a food processor or high powered blender to get a fine meal, flour-like texture

Here we wanted to go over our way of making raw coconut flour from coconut flakes. When we refer to coconut flour in our raw-unbaked recipes this is the coconut flour we are talking about (recipe below). Now this is completely different from the coconut flour that you see in stores. When we bake we use regular store bought coconut flour as it is processed more into a regular flour consistency.

Homemade raw coconut flour.

PURELY TWINS COCONUT FLOUR

HOW WE MAKE COCONUT FLOUR

Take your raw coconut flakes and place them into a food processor or high powered blender, and pulse until you get a fine meal, flour-like texture.

Basically you are just grinding down coconut flakes into a finer texture, and this is what we call raw coconut flour.

Again we only use this coconut flour version in our raw recipes not our cooked!

We love raw desserts!

PURELY RAW

We adore raw foods, not only for the health benefits (full of living enzymes to help make you feel vibrant and alive) but because of the flavor and texture. And hey, they are super easy to make up; most recipes can be made in minutes!

Raw foods can be enjoyed by everyone! Trust us, when you make our creamy chocolate cream cake you will have dairy lovers drooling for more! Did we mention our raw biscotti yet? Everyone who has had one can't get over how amazing they taste.

Over the years we have learned to find a balance of raw and cooked foods that works for us. We feel anyone can benefit from eating a little bit of raw goodness.

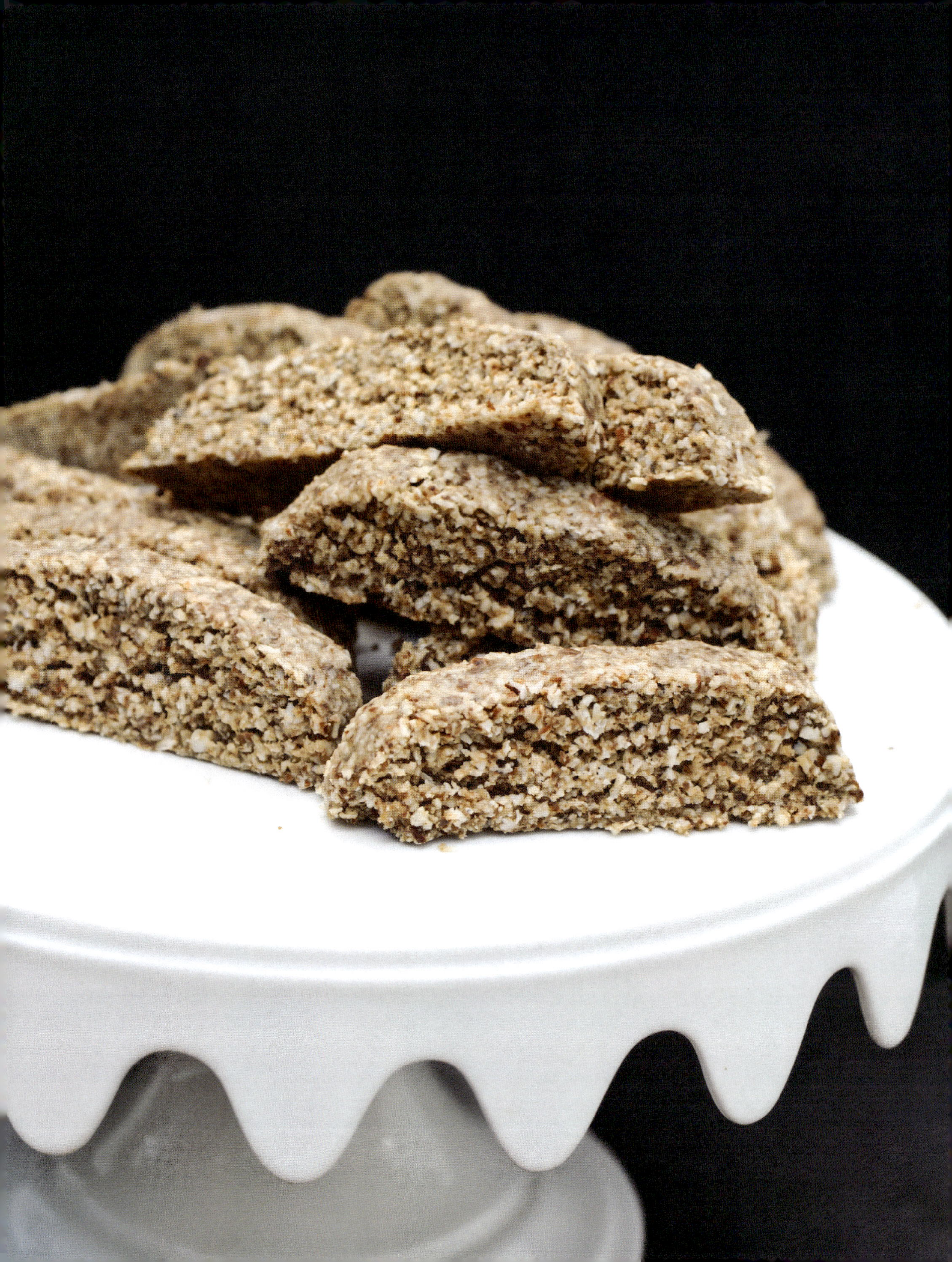

This was our very first raw biscotti that changed our life forever. The almonds and cardamom blend so perfectly together with a lingering hint of salt that completes the biscotti. This biscotti has a slightly crunchy outside with a soft chewy inside that provides a beautiful contrast that blends so nicely together.

Trust us it's hard to have just one!

ALMOND CARDAMOM BISCOTTI

Ingredients:
- 2 3/4 cups purelytwins almond flour (10oz)
- 1 cup purelytwins coconut flakes (3oz)
- 1/2 teaspoon sea salt
- 1 tablespoon cardamom powder
- 1/4 cup maple syrup (3oz)
- 1/3 cup coconut sugar (2oz)

MAKES 18-20 BISCOTTI

Place almond flour (p.43) and the coconut flakes (p.44) in a food processor. Pulse together to make semi-fine flour. Next add in sea salt, cardamom, coconut sugar and maple syrup. Pulse lightly until just combined as you do not want to over mix. You can also make this recipe by stirring all the ingredients in a bowl. This takes a little longer as it can be messy and sticky, so wearing food grade gloves helps. Once biscotti batter is starting to hold together, dump out biscotti batter onto tray or cutting board to start molding it into a long log shape. Next cut the log into biscotti shapes or any shape you desire.

Raw biscotti: Place biscotti slices on mesh-lined dehydrator tray. Dehydrate at 115 degrees for up to 60-72 hours or until desired dryness or texture is achieved.
We recommend using a food dehydrator for best results.

Baked biscotti: Place biscotti slices on a parchment lined cookie tray. Bake in oven at 300 degrees for 3-5 hours or until desired texture is achieved.
Note: baking gives the biscotti a golden brown color.

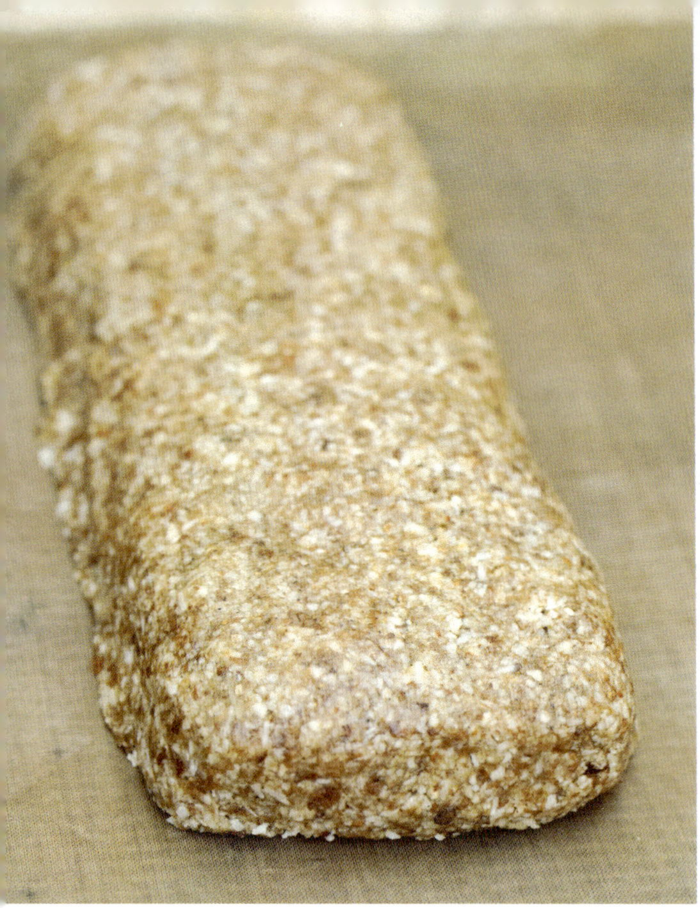
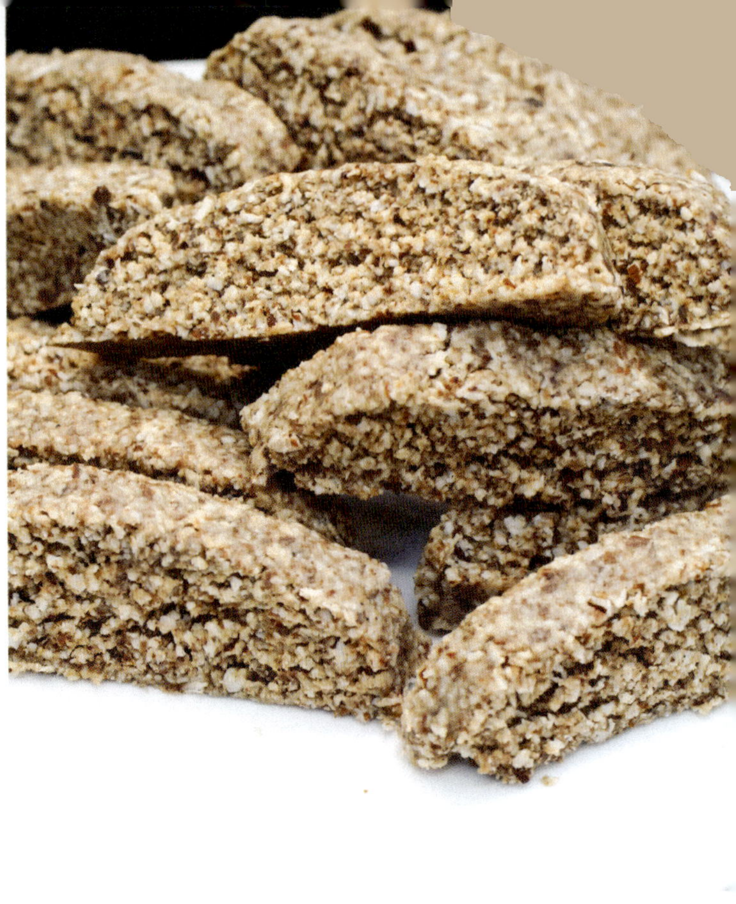
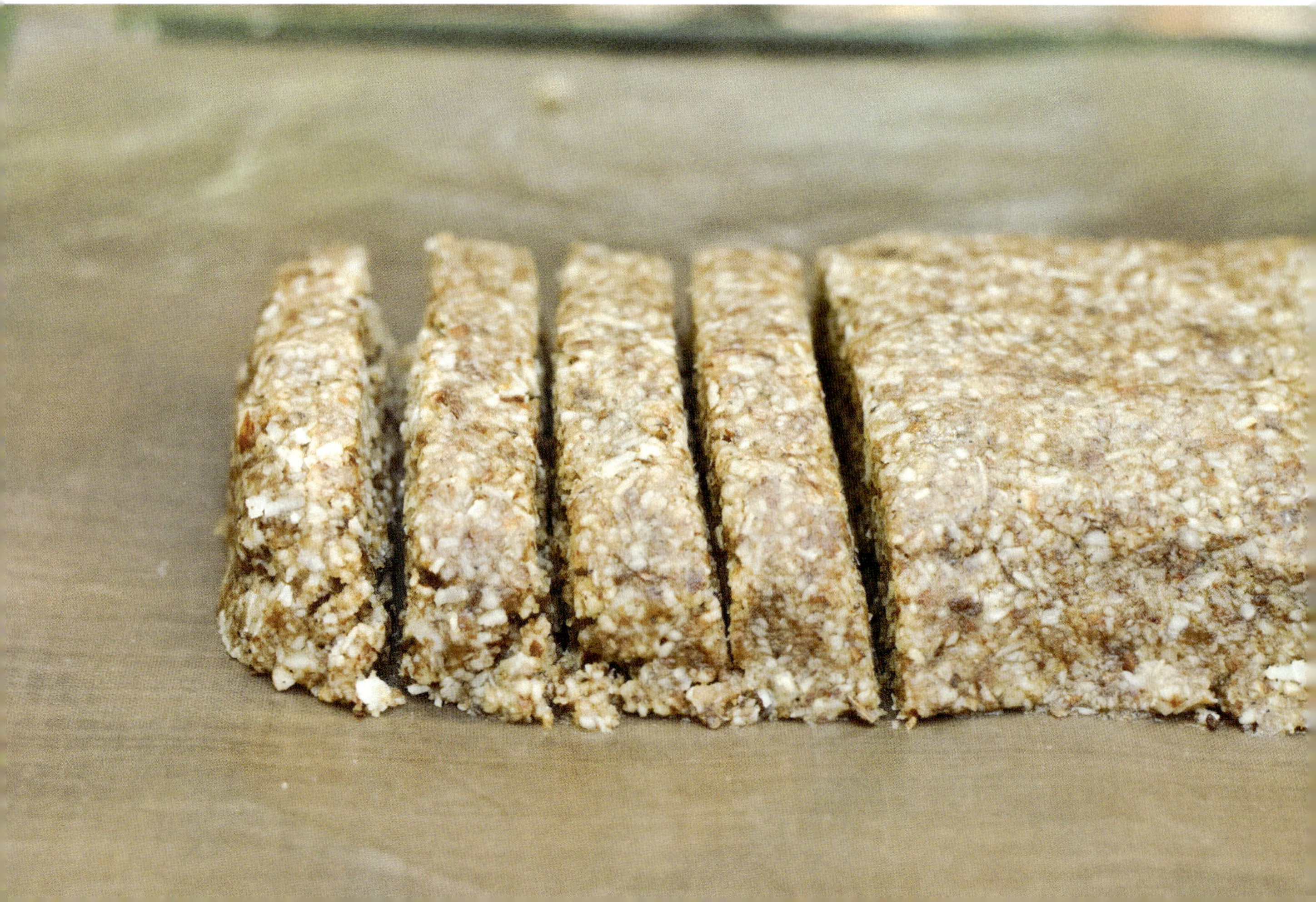

TIPS AND SUBSTITUTIONS

This biscotti recipe has not been tested with store bought nut meal, but we feel it would work in this recipe. You might have to adjust liquid sweetener so start slow when adding maple syrup.

It is recommended to soak almonds for easier digestion. Dry out almonds before making into flour. See page 43 for details for how to make purelytwins nut flours.

Can use regular coconut flakes that are not ground into a finer texture, but recipe works best if flakes are ground a little into flour.

For more of a low sugar biscotti use coconut nectar instead of maple syrup. Please note using coconut nectar provides for a more soft and chewy biscotti (does not get as hard and crunchy as the maple syrup version). And you might have to add 1 tbsp of water to help biscotti batter hold together.

Biscotti will get soft over time, we recommend to keep crunchy, store in refrigerator.

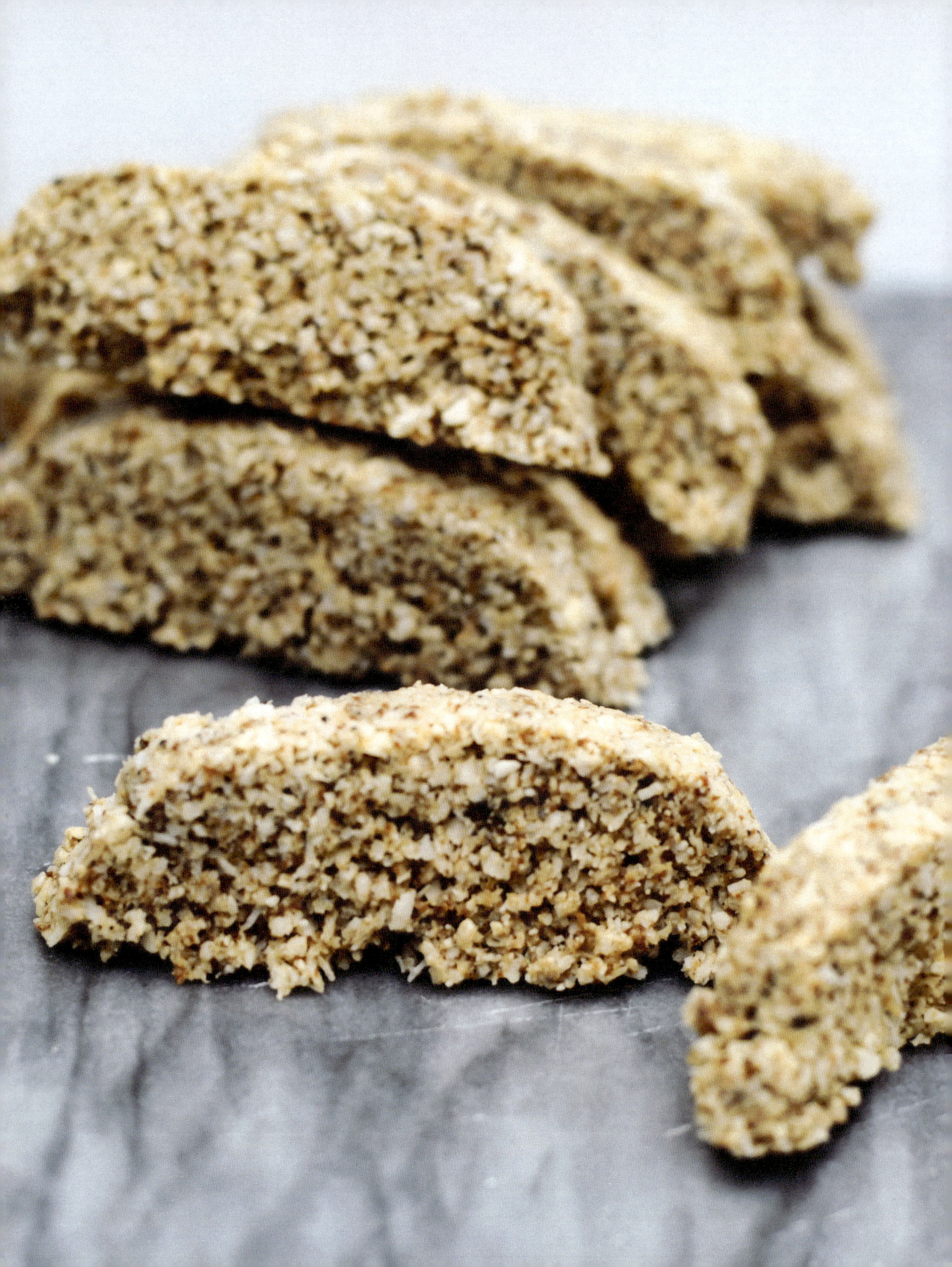

We are sharing our beloved cashew coconut biscotti with you so you can enjoy it in your own home as much as you want! Warning they are highly addictive, in a good way of course! Full of protein, healthy fats, and vitamins. We adore the texture and flavor from the cashews and coconut flakes. The right amount of sweetness that is so satisfying.

Our MOST popular biscotti flavor!!

CASHEW COCONUT BISCOTTI

Ingredients:
1 1/2 cups purelytwins cashew flour (6oz)
2 1/4 cups purelytwins coconut flour (7oz)
1/2 teaspoon sea salt
2 1/2 teaspoons vanilla bean powder
1/4 cup maple syrup (3oz)
1/3 cup coconut sugar (2oz)

MAKES 18-20 BISCOTTI

Make cashew flour (p.43) and coconut flour (p. 44). Place cashew and coconut flour in a food processor. Pulse together to make semi-fine flour. Next add in sea salt, vanilla bean powder, coconut sugar and maple syrup. Pulse lightly until just combined as you do not want to over mix. You can also make this recipe by stirring all the ingredients in a bowl. This takes a little longer as it can be messy and sticky, so wearing food grade gloves helps. Once biscotti batter is starting to hold together, dump out biscotti batter onto tray or cutting board to start molding it into a long log shape. Next cut the log into biscotti shapes or any shape you desire.

Raw biscotti: Place biscotti slices on mesh-lined dehydrator tray. Dehydrate at 115 degrees for up to 60-72 hours or until desired dryness or texture is achieved.
We recommend using a food dehydrator for best results.

Baked biscotti: Place biscotti slices on a parchment lined cookie tray. Bake in oven at 300 degrees for 3-5 hours or until desired texture is achieved.
Note: baking gives the biscotti a golden brown color.

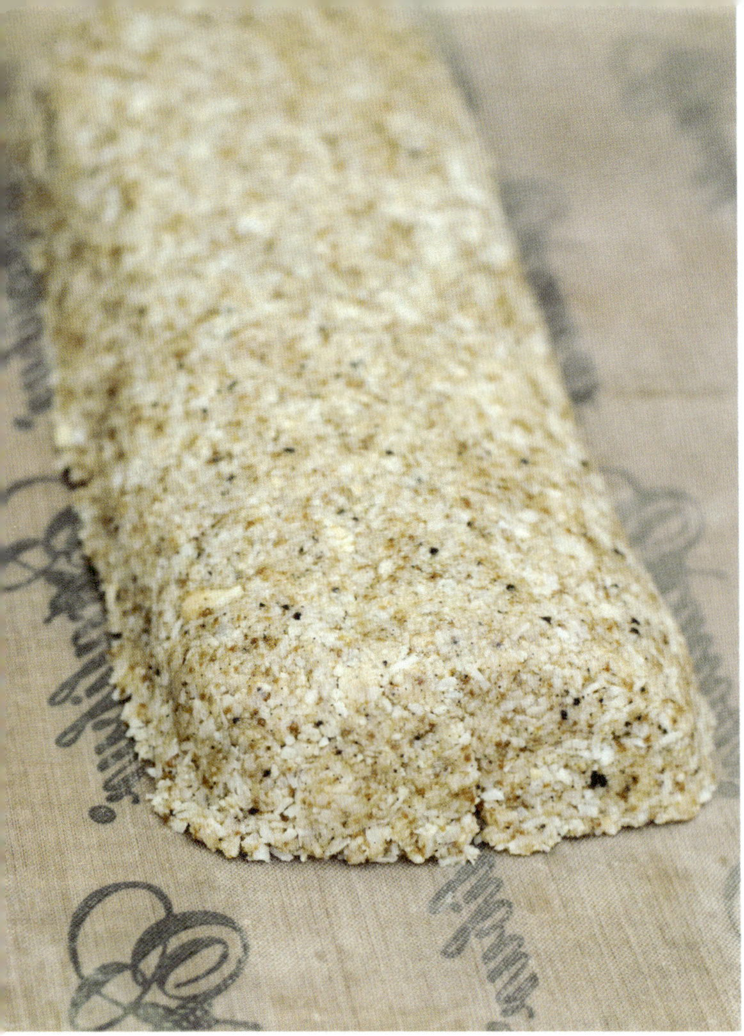

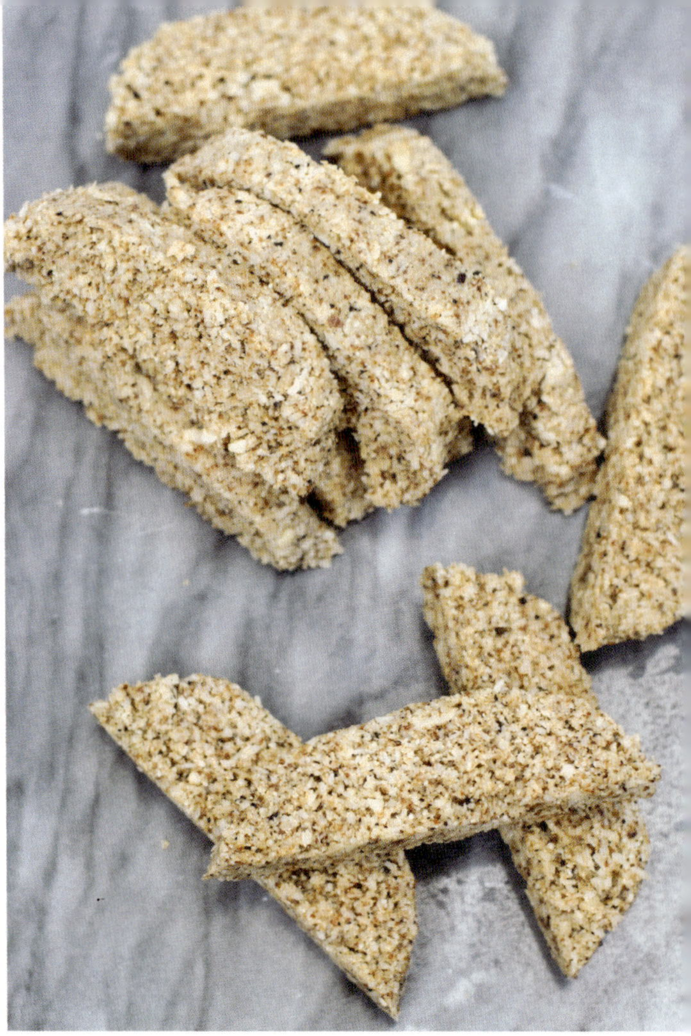

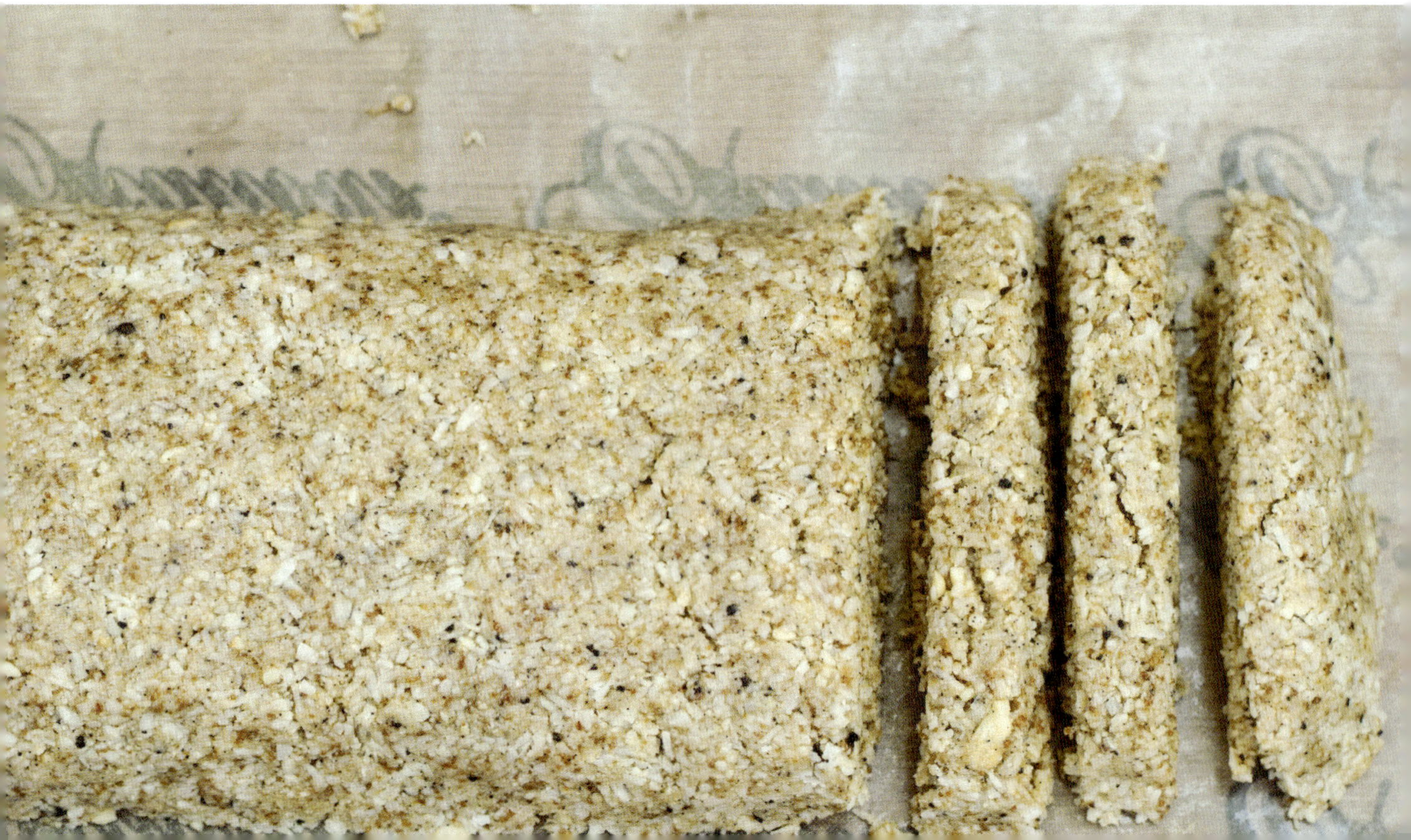

TIPS AND SUBSTITUTIONS

This biscotti recipe has not been tested with store bought nut meal, but we feel it would work in this recipe. You might have to adjust liquid sweetener so start slow when adding maple syrup.

It is recommended to soak almonds for easier digestion. Dry out almonds before making into flour. See page 43 for details for how to make purelytwins nut flours.

Can use regular coconut flakes that are not ground into a finer texture, but recipe works best if flakes are ground a little into flour.

For more of a low sugar biscotti use coconut nectar instead of maple syrup. Please note using coconut nectar provides for a more soft and chewy biscotti (does not get as hard and crunchy as the maple syrup version). And you might have to add 1 tbsp of water to help biscotti batter hold together.

Biscotti will get soft over time, we recommend to keep crunchy, store in refrigerator.

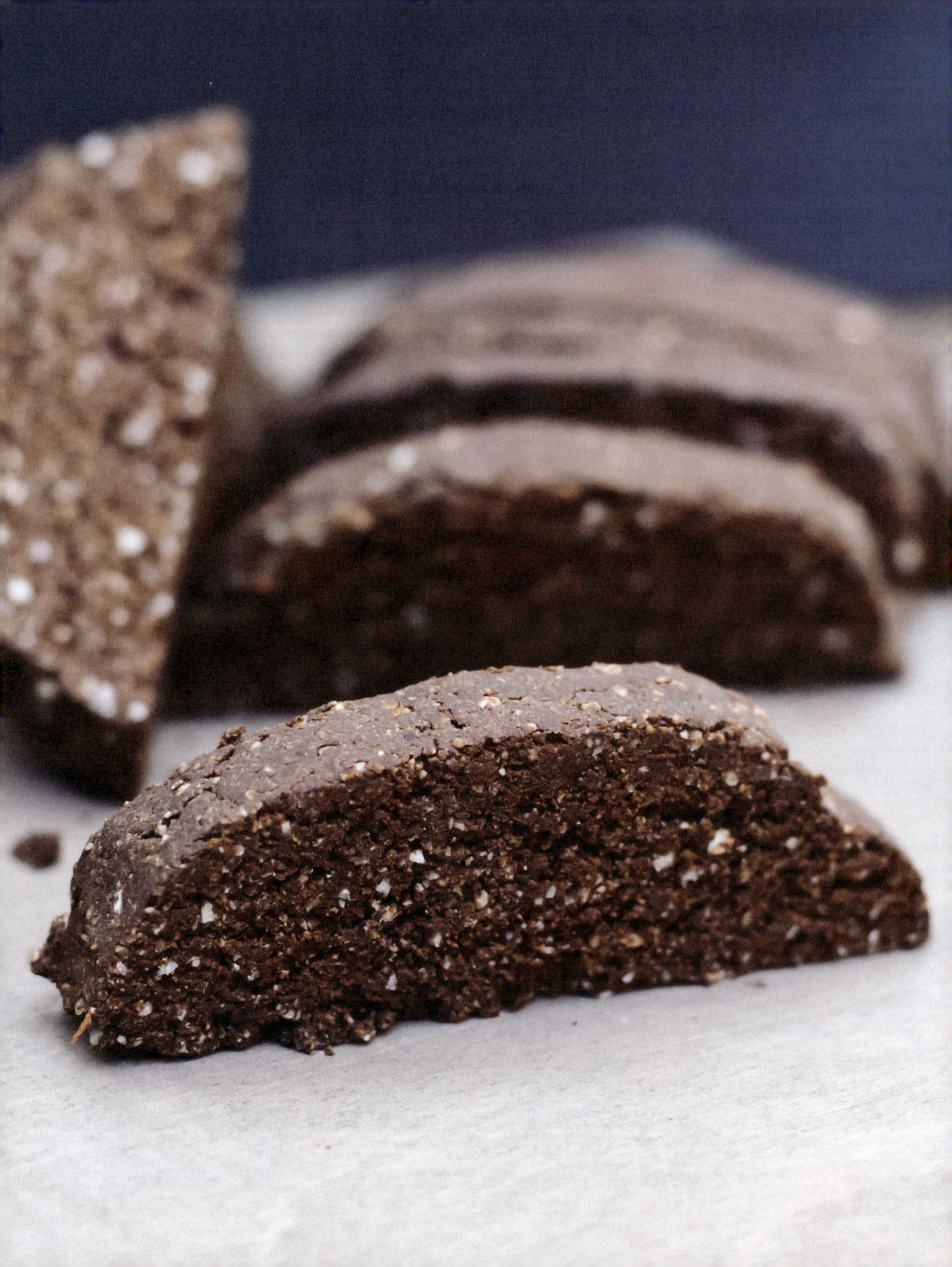

We made this biscotti because we wanted some way to enjoy chocolate with our morning coffee. This biscotti batter is very easy to work with compared to other biscotti recipes. The mesquite flavor brings more depth to the flavor.

Crunchy, chocolately goodness!

CHOCOLATE MESQUITE BISCOTTI

Ingredients:
2 1/3 cups purelytwins hazelnut meal (9oz)
1/4 cup + 3 tbsp mesquite (2oz)
3/4 cup raw cacao powder (3oz)
1/2 teaspoon sea salt
2 teaspoons cinnamon
1/4 + 3 tbsp cup maple syrup (4 1/2oz)
1/3 cup coconut sugar (2oz)

MAKES 18-20 BISCOTTI

Make hazelnut flour (p.43). Then place in food processor with mesquite and cacao powder. Pulse together to make semi-fine flour. Next add in sea salt, cinnamon, coconut sugar and maple syrup. Pulse lightly until just combined as you do not want to over mix. You can also make this recipe by stirring all the ingredients in a bowl. This takes a little longer as it can be messy and sticky, so wearing food grade gloves helps. Once biscotti batter is starting to hold together, dump out biscotti batter onto tray or cutting board to start molding it into a long log shape. Next cut the log into biscotti shapes or any shape you desire.

Raw biscotti: Place biscotti slices on mesh-lined dehydrator tray. Dehydrate at 115 degrees for up to 60-72 hours or until desired dryness or texture is achieved.
We recommend using a food dehydrator for best results.

Baked biscotti: Place biscotti slices on a parchment lined cookie tray. Bake in oven at 300 degrees for 3-5 hours or until desired texture is achieved.
Note: baking gives the biscotti a golden brown color.

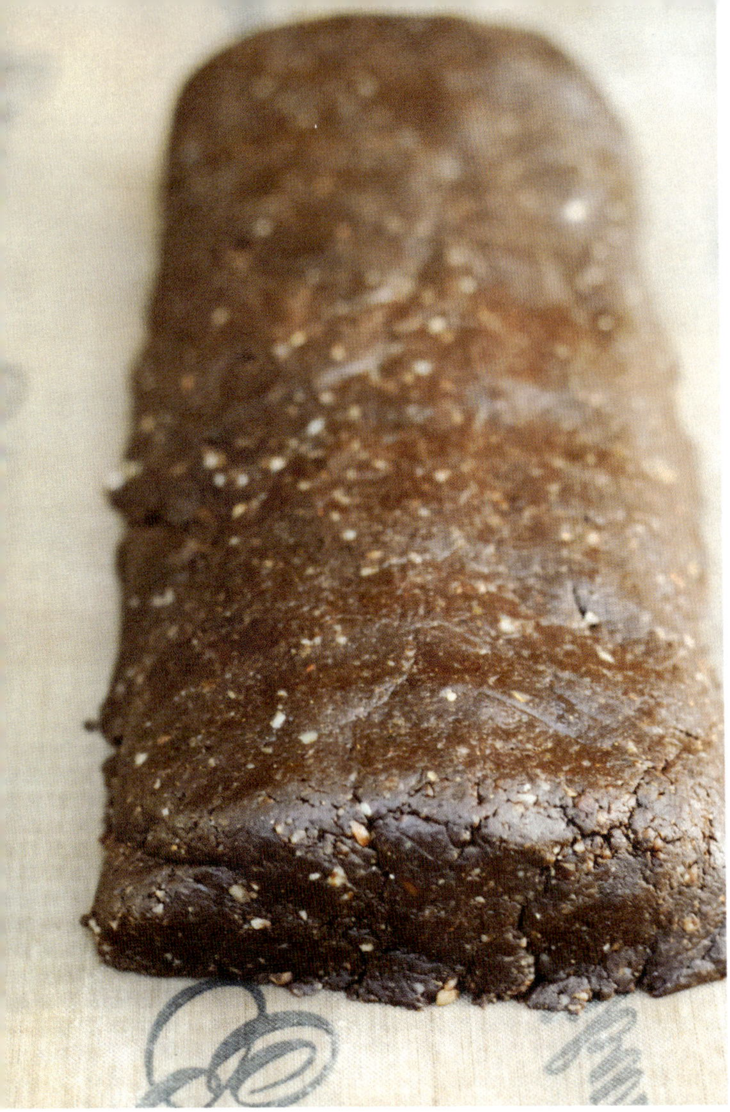

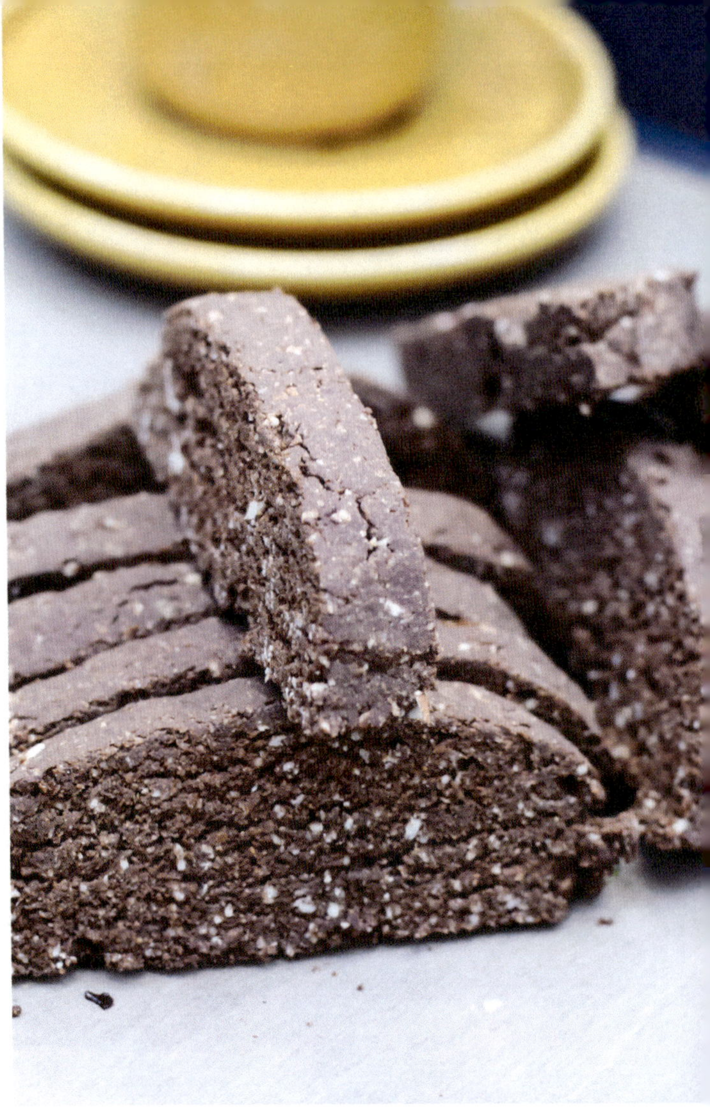

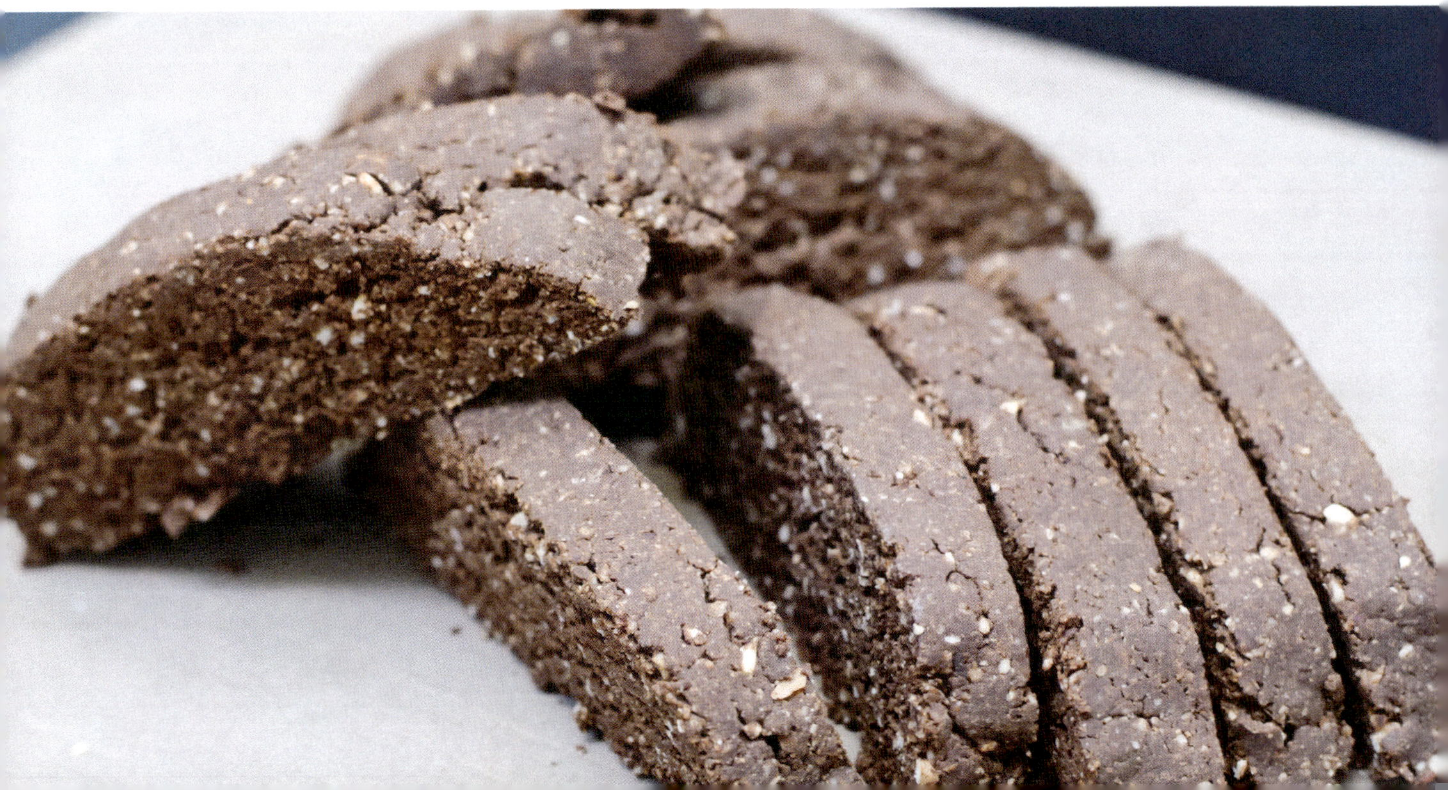

TIPS AND SUBSTITUTIONS

This biscotti recipe has not been tested with store bought nut meal, but we feel it would work in this recipe. You might have to adjust liquid sweetener so start slow when adding maple syrup.

It is recommended to soak hazelnuts for easier digestion. Dry out hazelnuts before making into flour. See page 43 for details for how to make purelytwins nut flours. Can use purelytwins almond flour instead of the hazelnut flour.

If you do not have mesquite, you can replace with carob powder or more nut flour. For more of a low sugar biscotti use coconut nectar instead of maple syrup. Please note using coconut nectar provides for a more soft and chewy biscotti (does not get as hard and crunchy as the maple syrup version). And you might have to add 1 tbsp of water to help biscotti batter hold together.

Biscotti will get soft over time, we recommend to keep crunchy, store in refrigerator.

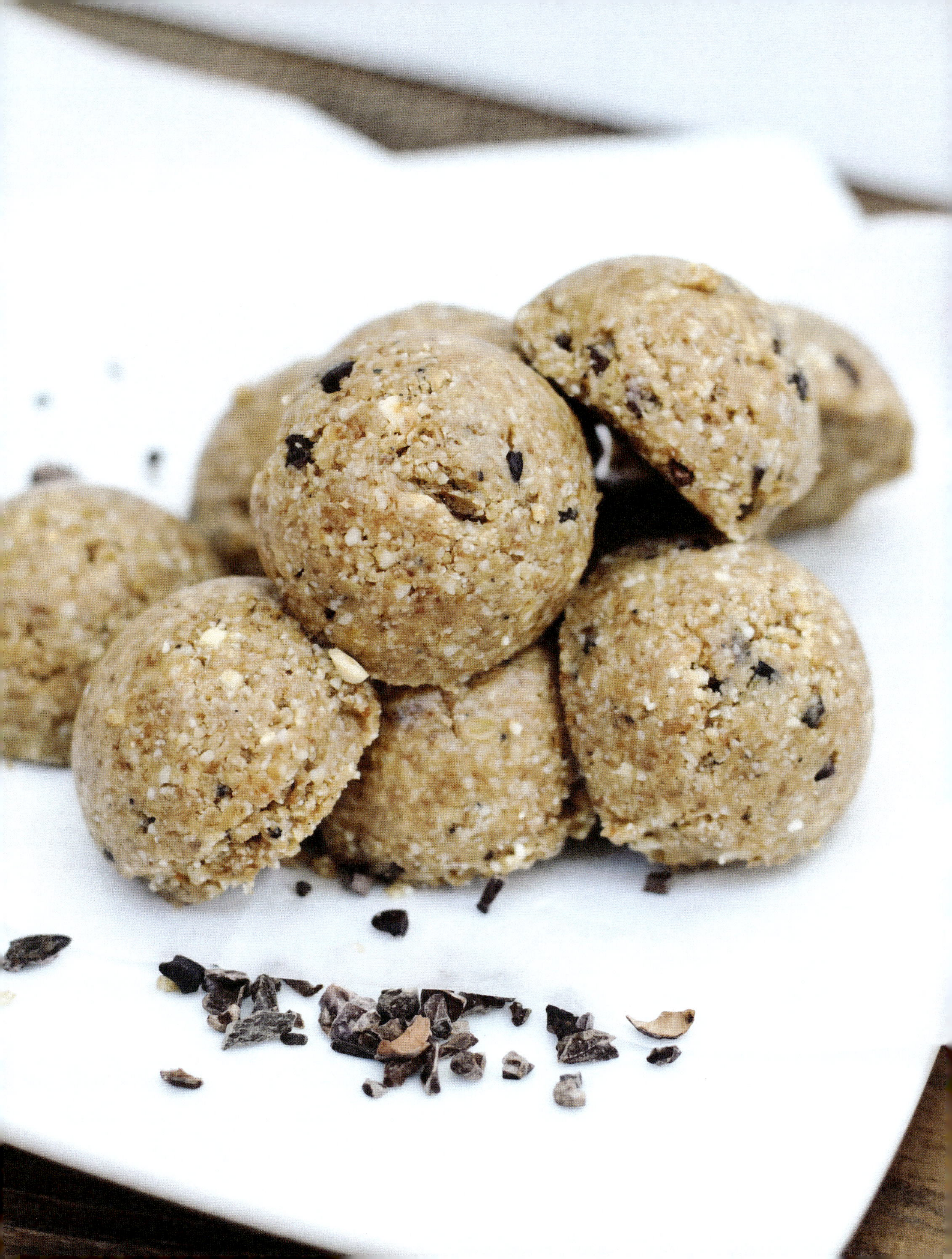

We adore the nutty flavor that the flax meal gives these dough balls along with the espresso-like flavor from the cacao nibs. A perfect way to enjoy raw cookie dough on a daily basis. We love lucuma and the little extra sweetness in flavor it brings. Store these in freezer so you always have some raw cookies to enjoy when the urge hits.

Our favorite raw dough ball!

CASHEW NIB DOUGH BALLS

Ingredients:
1 cup purelytwins cashew flour (4 1/2 oz)
2 tablespoons lucuma (1/2 oz)
2 tablespoons flax meal (1/2 oz)
1/8 teaspoon vanilla bean powder
2 tablespoons coconut sugar
2 tablespoons coconut oil, liquid (1oz)
3 tablespoons coconut nectar (2 1/4oz)

MAKES ABOUT 10 DOUGH BALLS

First make cashew flour (p.43). Next place all dry ingredients into a large bowl and stir together. You could also do this in a Vita-mix blender or food processor for finer dough balls.

Then start adding wet ingredients (coconut oil and coconut nectar). Continue to stir until batter comes together. Then scoop with cookie scooper or tablespoon onto mesh-lined dehydrator tray.

May eat raw as is or dehydrate at 110 degrees for 4-6 hours. You could bake this at 350 degrees in oven for 5-10 minutes, or until desired texture is achieved. Store in refrigerator or freezer.

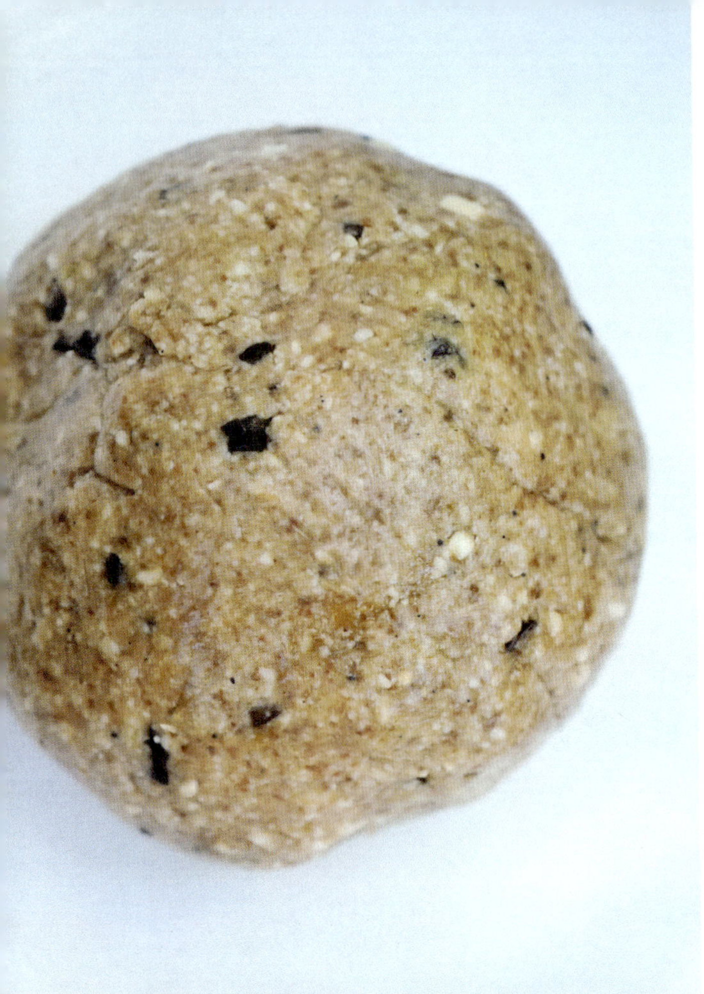
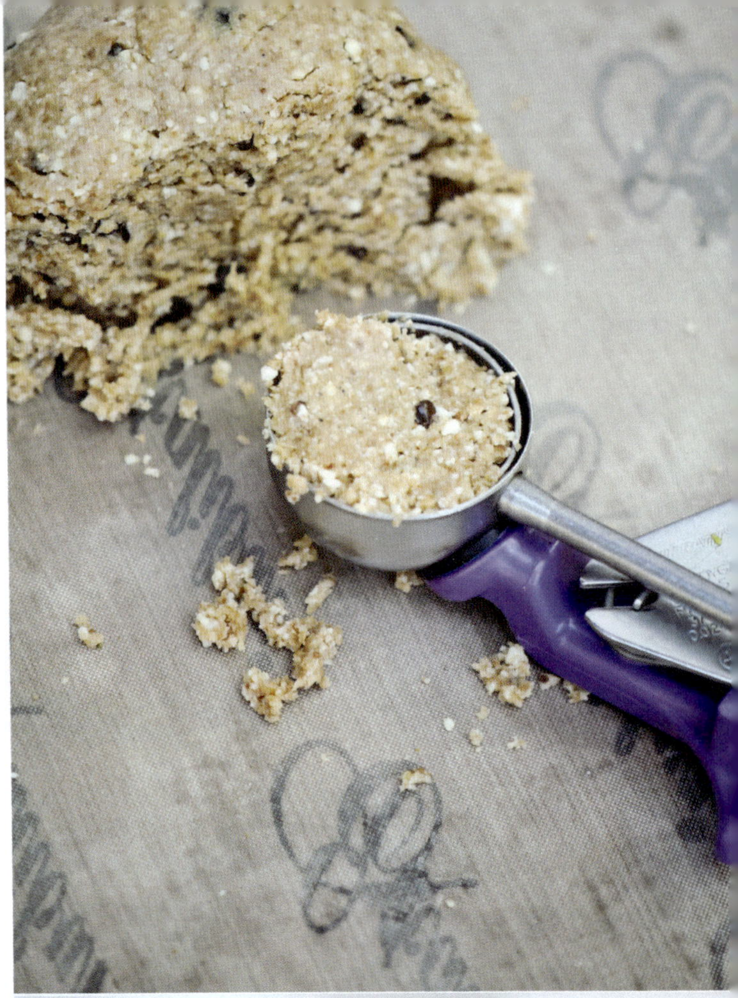
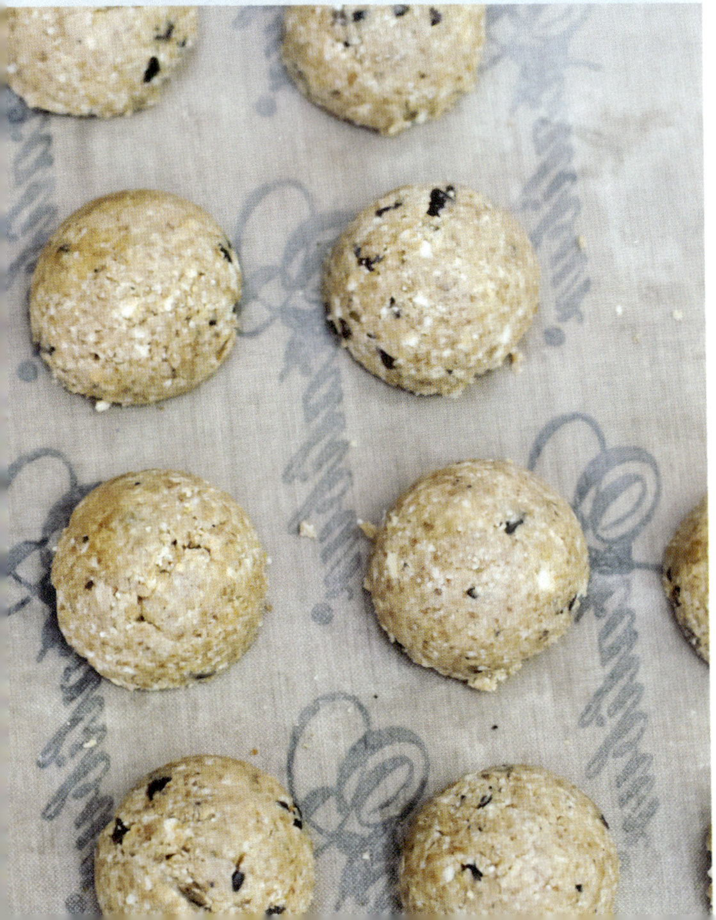
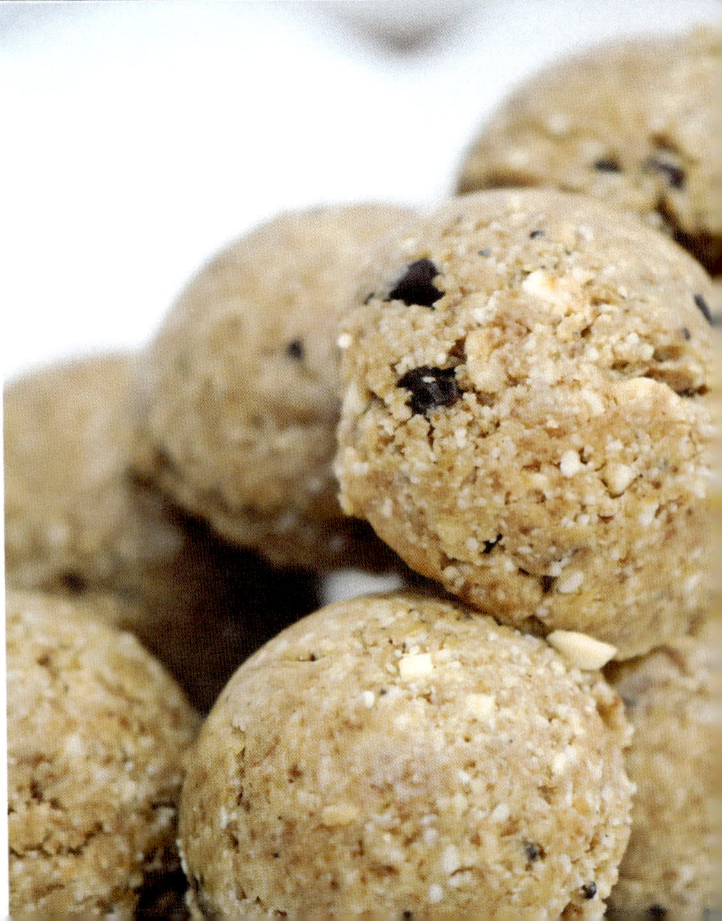

TIPS AND SUBSTITUTIONS

It is recommended to soak cashews for easier digestion. Dry out cashews before making into flour. See page 43 for details for how to make purelytwins nut flours.
If you do not have lucuma you can use your favorite protein powder or add more cashew flour or another nut flour.
If you do not have vanilla bean powder can use 1-2 tsp vanilla extract.
Can use honey or maple syrup instead of the coconut nectar.
Chocolate chips can be used instead of cacao nibs, which will also make it taste more like a raw chocolate chip cookie dough!
You can omit the flax meal all together if you would like, we just like the additional health benefits of it. You could replace with more cashew flour.

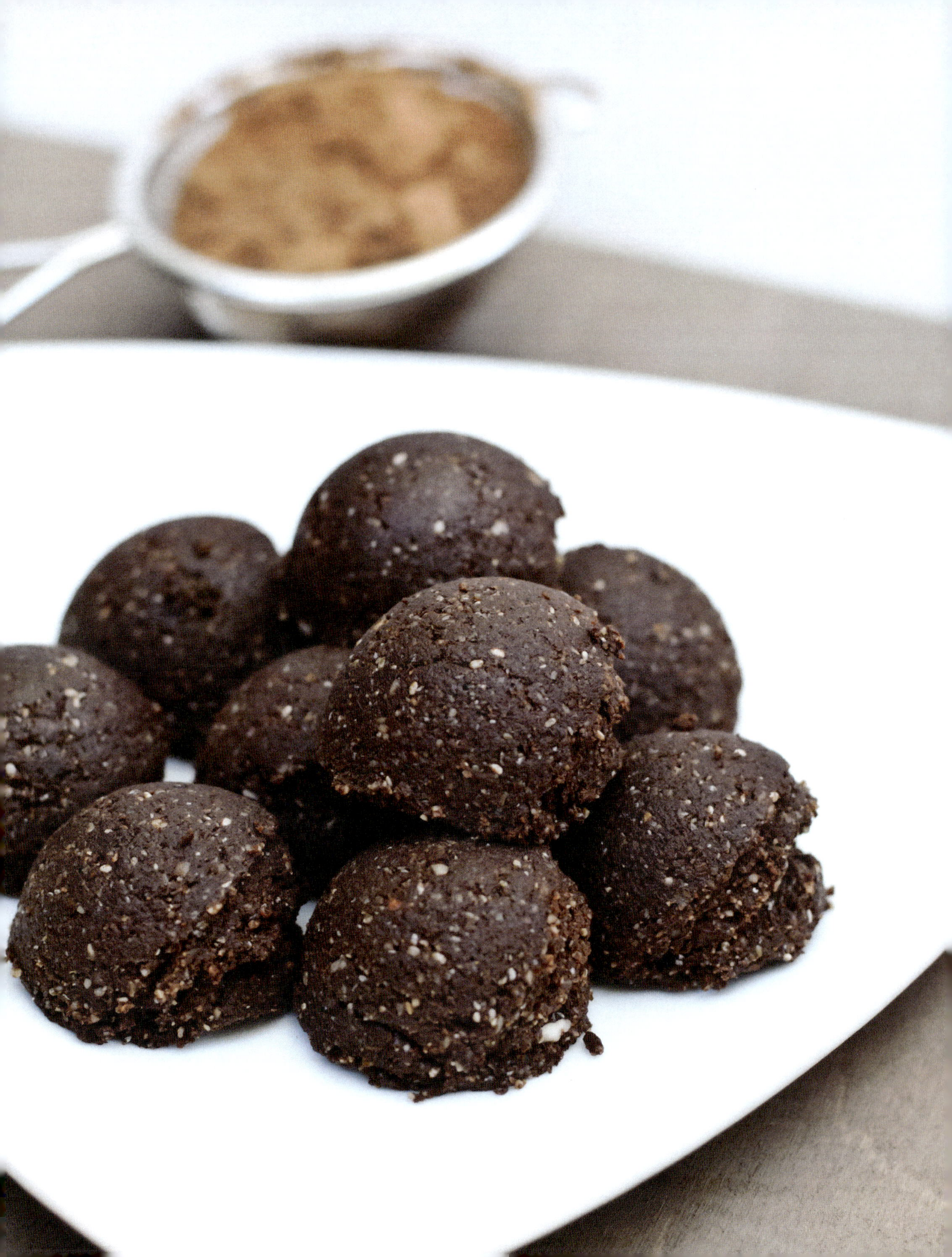

One of our popular raw dough balls that we used to sell online. We adore the heat from the cayenne mixed with the earthy blend of hazelnuts + cacao together. We added chia seeds for an additional nutritional boost in fiber and Omega 3's. A nutrient dense soft cookie dough ball with a kick.

A little spice in every bite!

SPICED COCOA DOUGH BALLS

Ingredients:
1 cup purelytwins hazelnut flour (3 1/2)
6 tablespoons cacao (1oz)
2 tablespoons chia seed flour (1/2oz)
1/2 teaspoons cinnamon
1/8 teaspoon cayenne
2 tablespoons coconut sugar
2 tablespoons coconut oil, liquid form (1oz)
3 tablepoons coconut nectar (2 1/4oz)

MAKES ABOUT 10 DOUGH BALLS

First make your hazelnut flour (p.43). We grind our whole chia seeds in a coffee grinder making it like flour, or you can leave them whole. Next place all dry ingredients into a large bowl and stir together. You could also do this in a Vita-mix blender or food processor for finer dough balls.

Then start adding wet ingredients (coconut oil and coconut nectar). Continue to stir until batter comes together. Then scoop with cookie scooper or tablespoon onto mesh-lined dehydrator tray.

May eat raw as is or dehydrate at 110 degrees for 4-6 hours. You could bake this at 350 degrees in oven for 5-10 minutes, or until desired texture is achieved. Store in refrigerator or freezer.

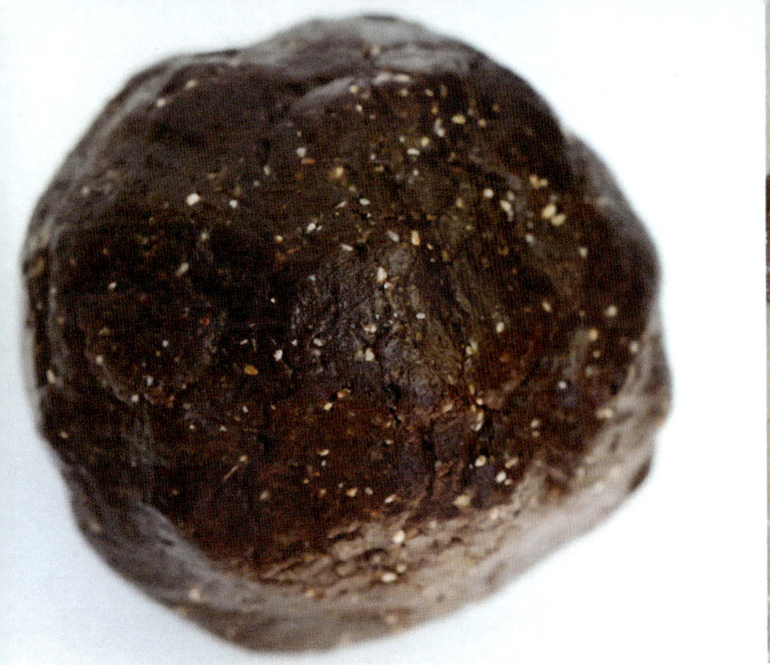
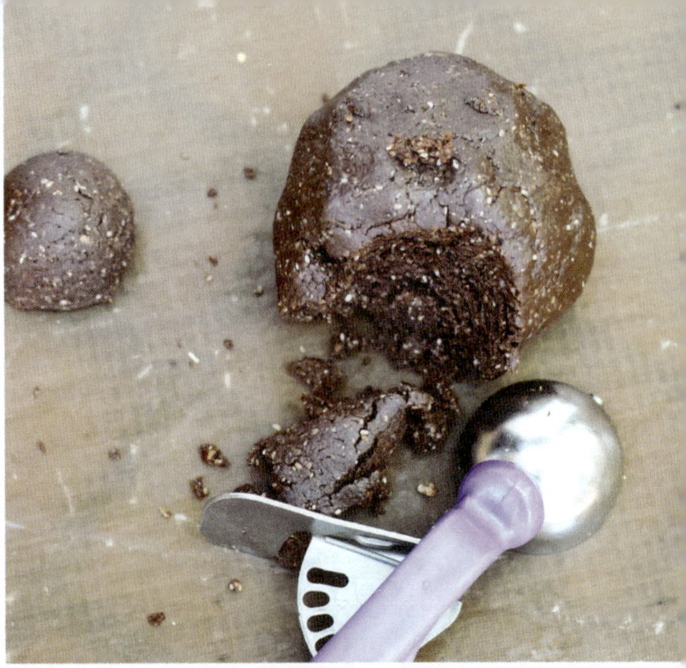
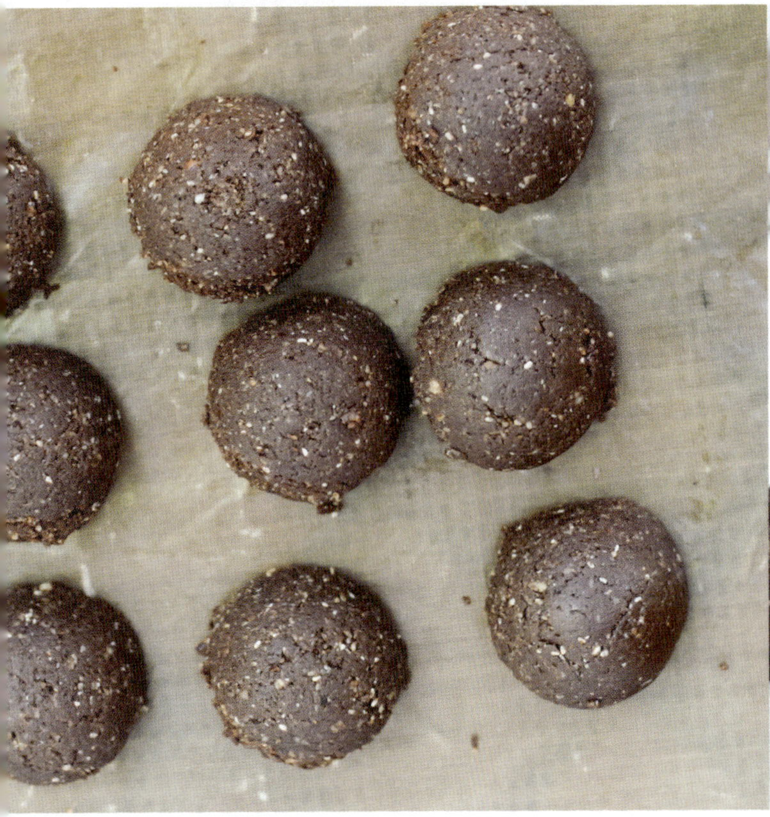
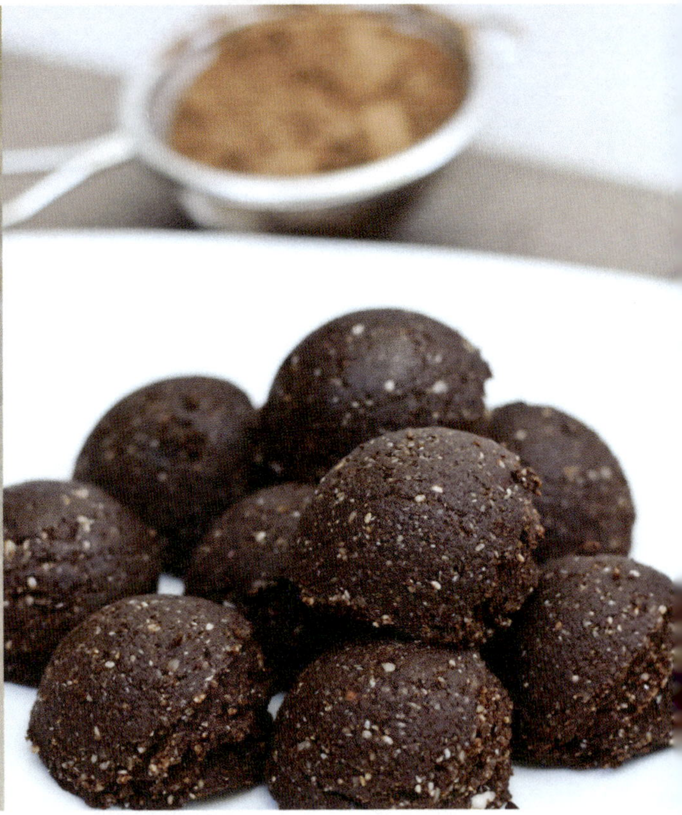
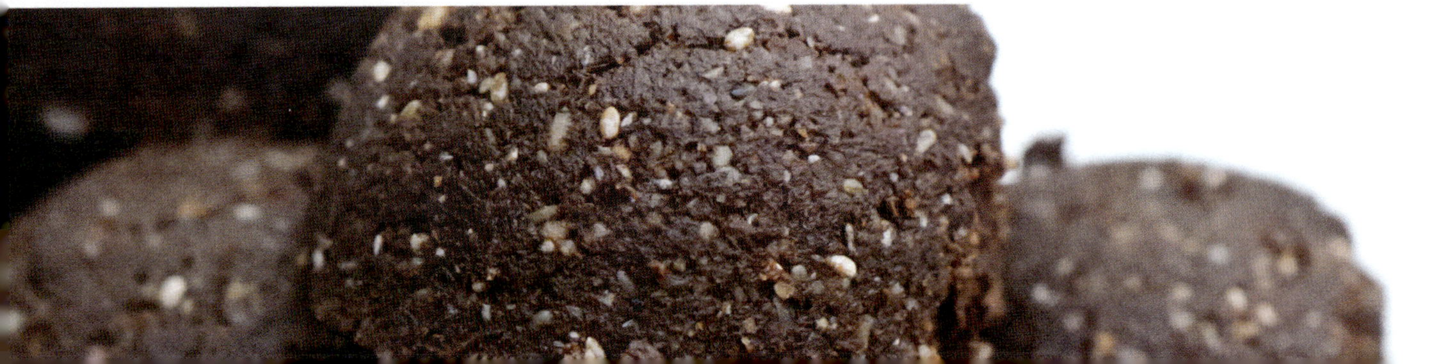

TIPS AND SUBSTITUTIONS

It is recommended to soak hazelnuts for easier digestion. Dry out hazelnuts before making into flour. See page 43 for details for how to make purelytwins nut flours.
You could use any nut meal in this recipe instead of hazelnuts.
Can use carob powder instead of cacao if you cannot have chocolate.
Can use honey or maple syrup instead of the coconut nectar.
You can omit the chia seeds all together if you would like, we just like the additional health benefits of them. You could replace with more nut meal.

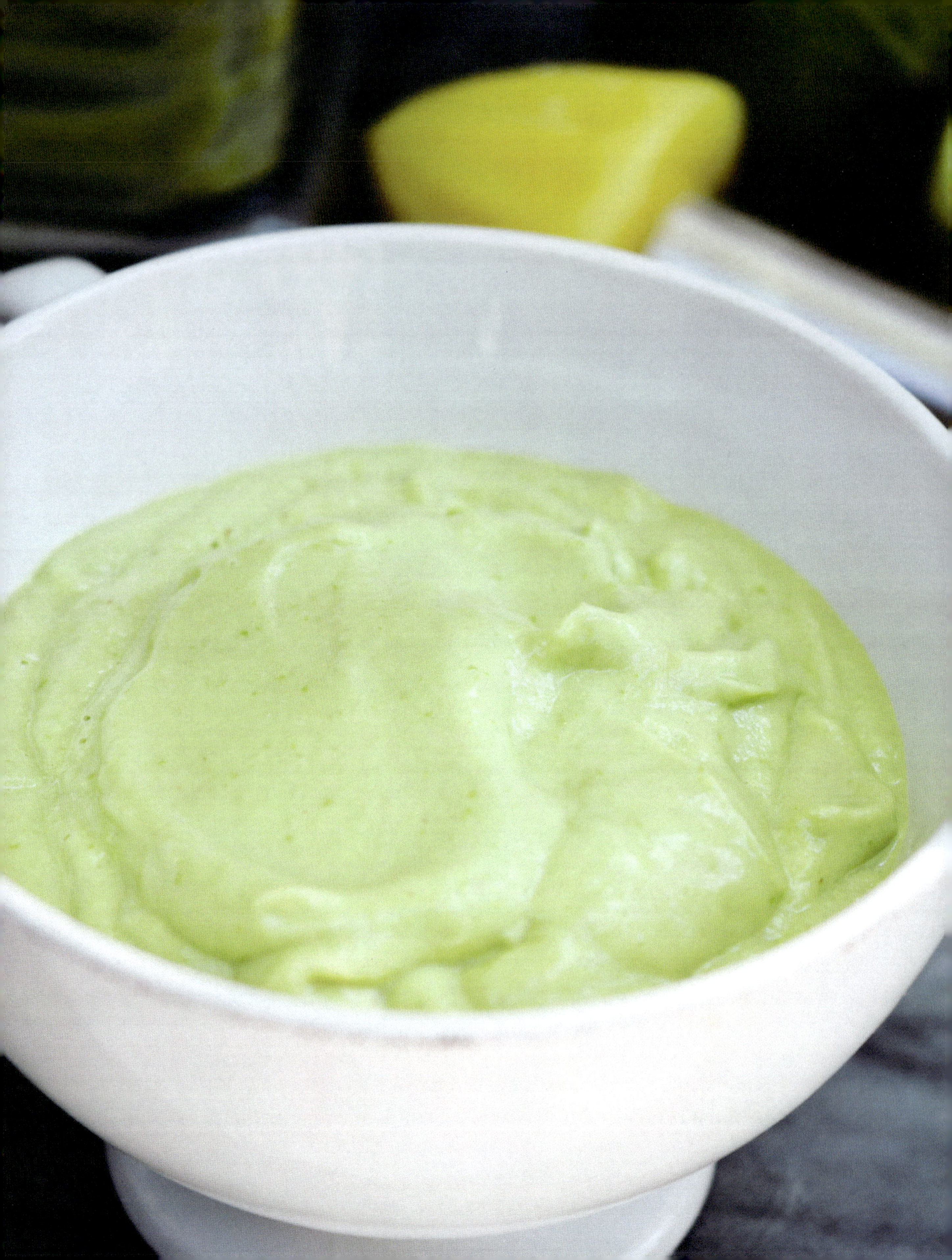

There is no denying how much we love our avocados! They make the best base for rich and creamy puddings and frostings. We have shown pictures of us enjoying plenty of avocado puddings on our blog! We just love them! Avocados are a great way to stay full and satisfied. Limes are great for fat burning too! A nice bonus.

A yummy fat-burning pudding!

Key Lime Avocado Pudding

Ingredients:
- 1 Hass avocado, medium/large
- 1/2 cup chopped cucumber, lightly skinned
- 15 drops liquid stevia
- 2 large zest of limes
- 4-5 tablespoons fresh lime juice

Serves 1

Cut avocado and lightly skin cucumber. Place avocado and cucumber into blender along with stevia, lime zest and juice. Blend until smooth and creamy.

This recipe can be doubled for a larger batch. You can omit the cucumber; we just like adding it for more volume to our pudding. You can add more or less depending on the consistency you want for your pudding.

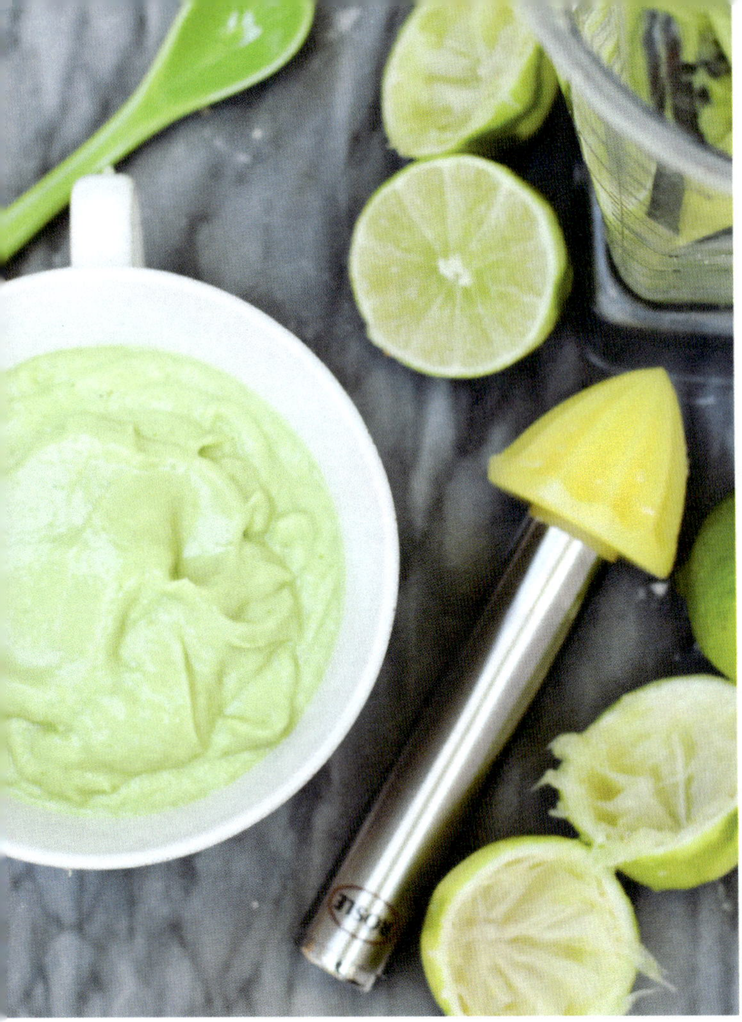
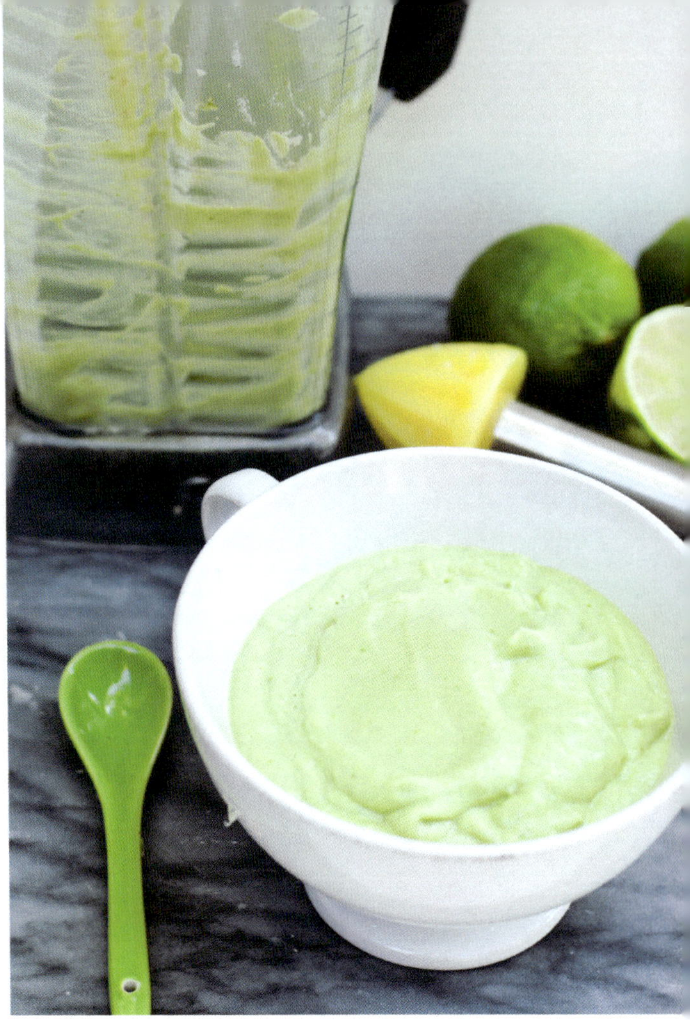
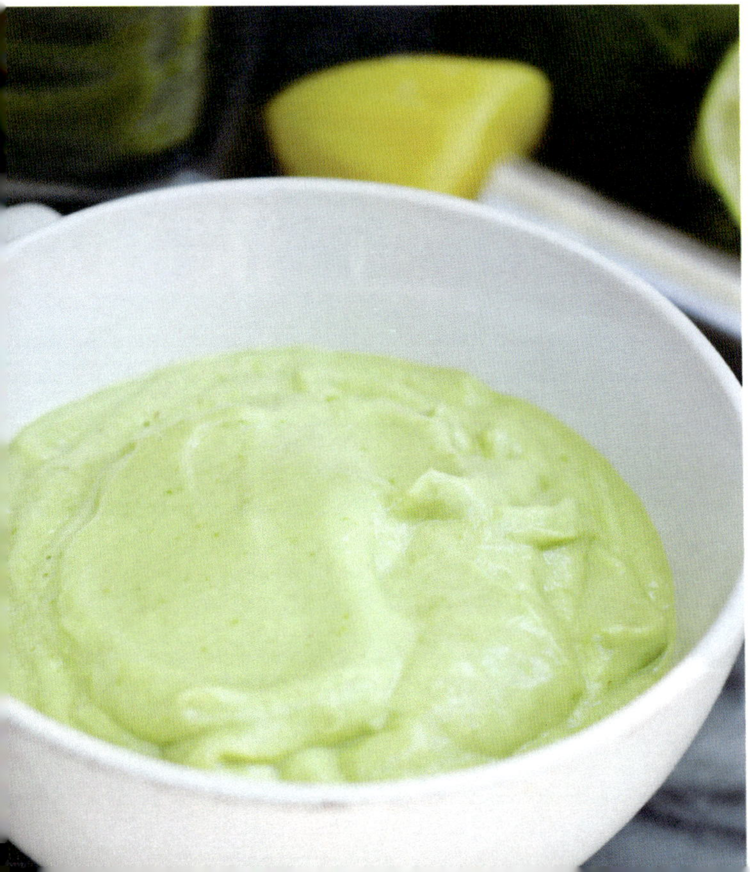
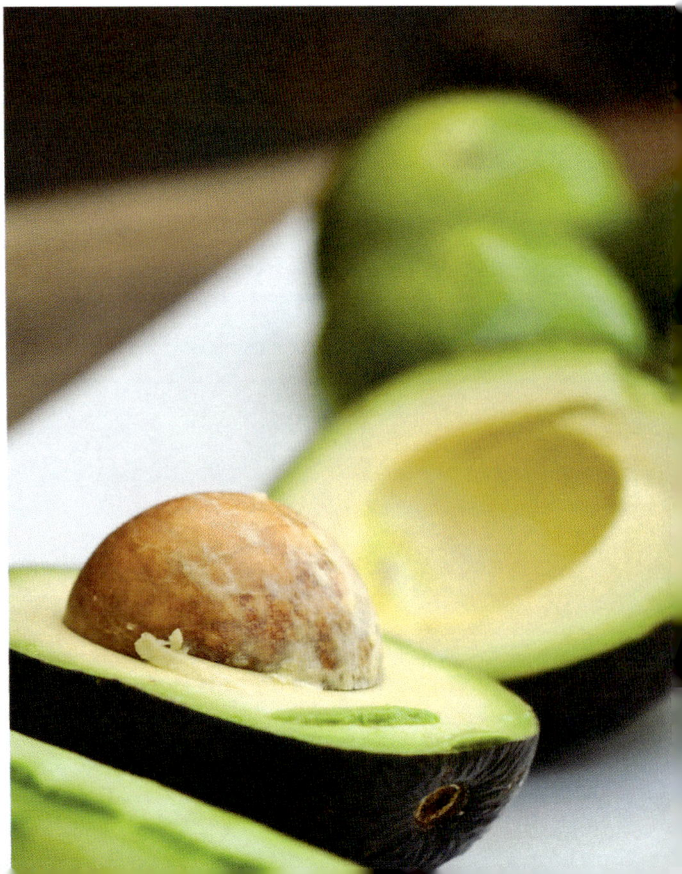

TIPS AND SUBSTITUTIONS

If you are not a fan of lime, you can use lemon for another light and wonderful balance of flavors.

For a more nutritional boost toss in some spinach or kale to your pudding. Adjust flavor and sweetness level to taste.

If not a fan of stevia, you can omit and use 1 small banana (or add more until desired sweetness is achieved). Or can use 1-2 tbsp of your favorite sweetener.

This avocado pudding is an easy basic pudding base that you can now adjust to your liking!

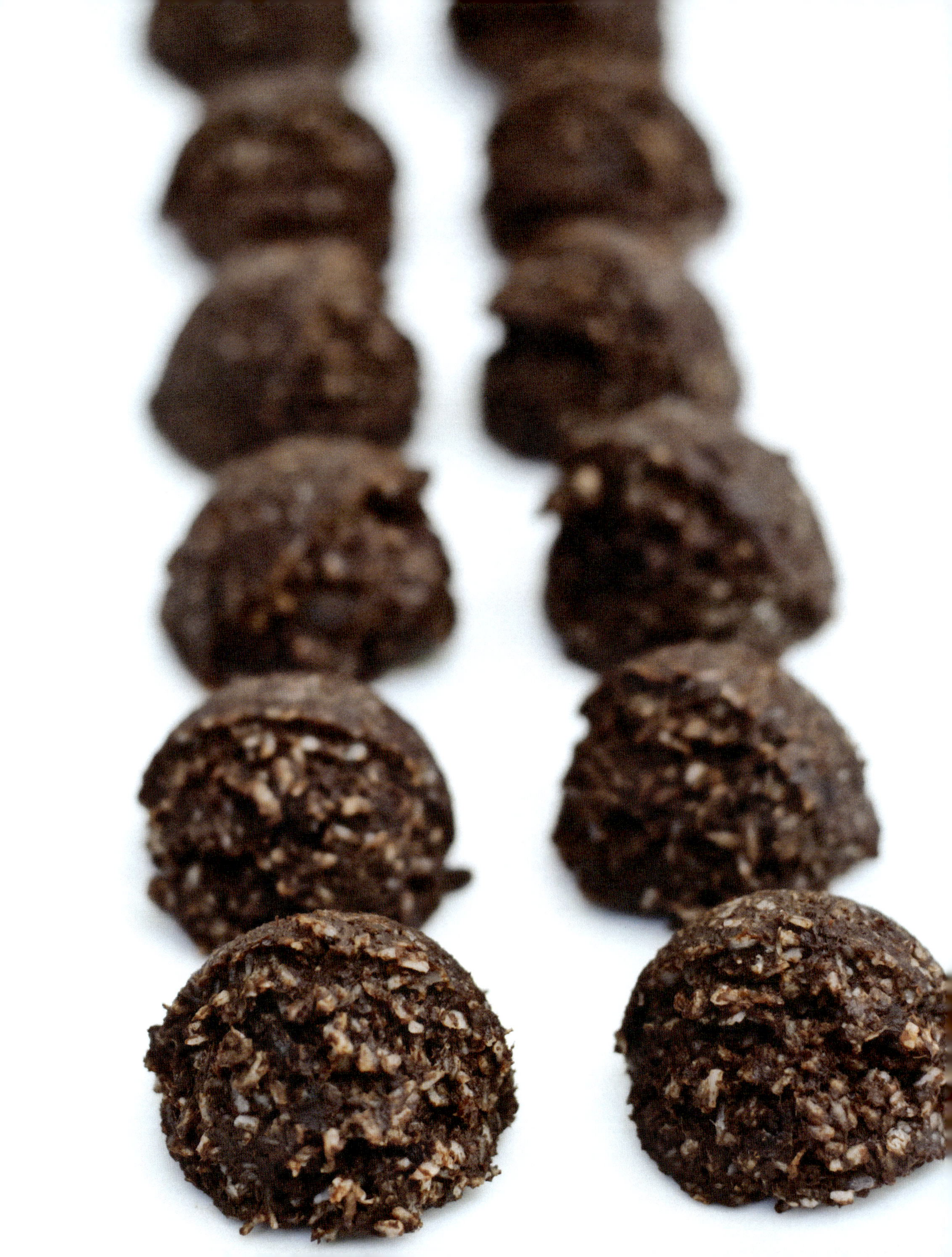

We love the texture and sweetness that the dates provide these chewy coconut macaroons. If you leave date paste a little chunky you get some extra chewiness in each macaroon. Nothing like dates and chocolate together.

Chewy, with a little sweetness in every bite!

CHOCOLATE DATE MACAROONS

Ingredients:
1/2 cup cacao powder (1 3/4oz)
1 1/2 cups coconut flakes (5oz)
3 tablespoons coconut oil, liquid (1 1/2oz)
3/4 cup date paste (7 1/2oz)
2 teaspoons vanilla extract
pinch sea salt (optional)

Makes 21-22 macaroons

Need to make date paste (p. 42).
Place cacao powder, coconut flakes, vanilla and sea salt (optional) in a large bowl. Stir together. Scoop out date paste and place into bowl of dry ingredients. Continue to stir. Batter will be thick depending on how thick date paste was. Add in coconut oil. Stir until all combined. Scoop with cookie scooper or spoon. Amount you make will vary on size of scoop.

You may enjoy as is or dehydrate for 5-10 hours at 110 degrees. Store in refrigerator or freezer.

*Note: You can make in a mixer or make these macaroons in a food processor and pulse lightly until combined.

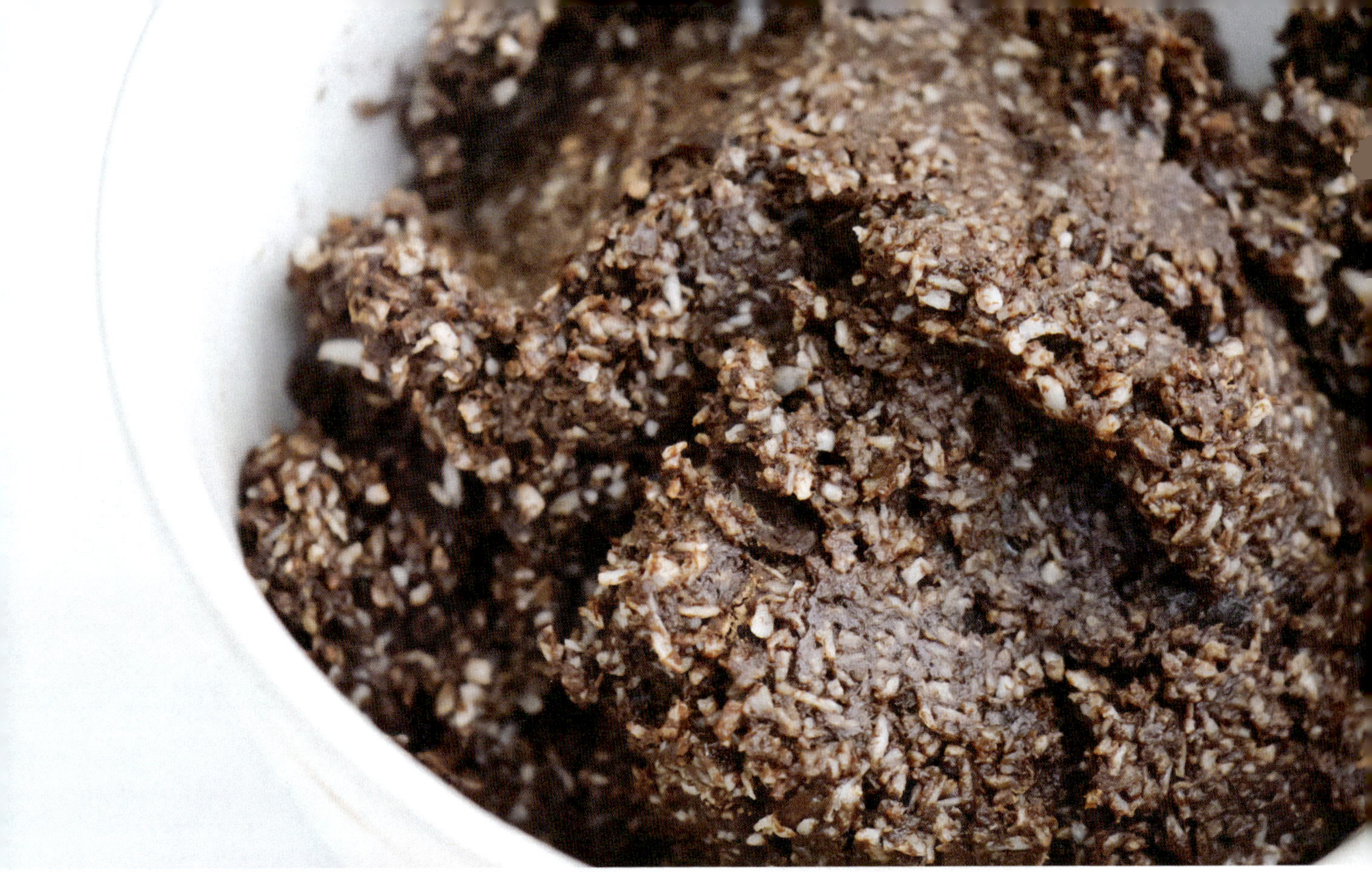

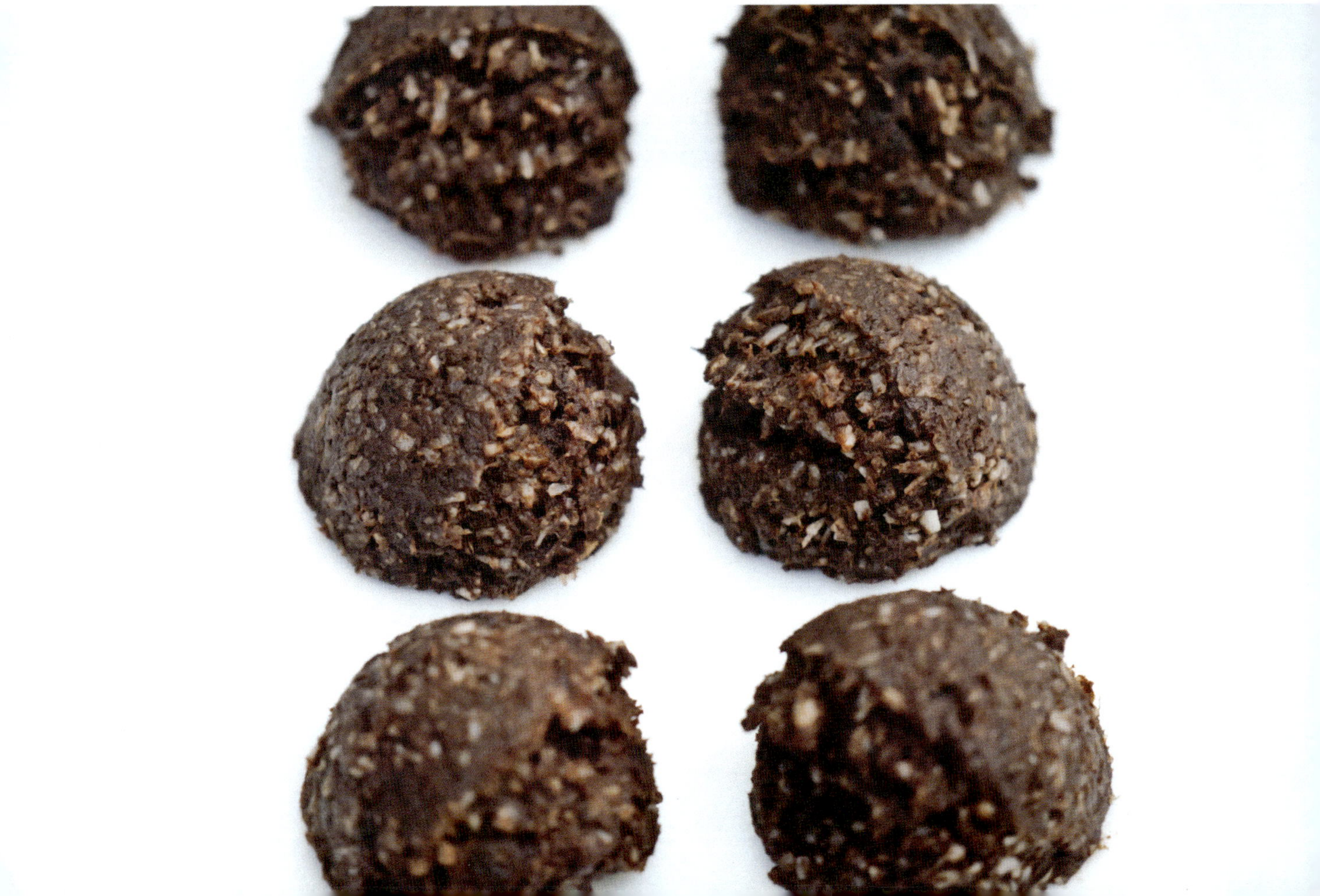

TIPS AND SUBSTITUTIONS

Can use carob powder instead of cacao powder.
If you do not have date paste, replace with liquid sweetener of choice like honey, maple or coconut nectar.
If using date paste and not sweet enough we suggest adding in some drops of liquid stevia.

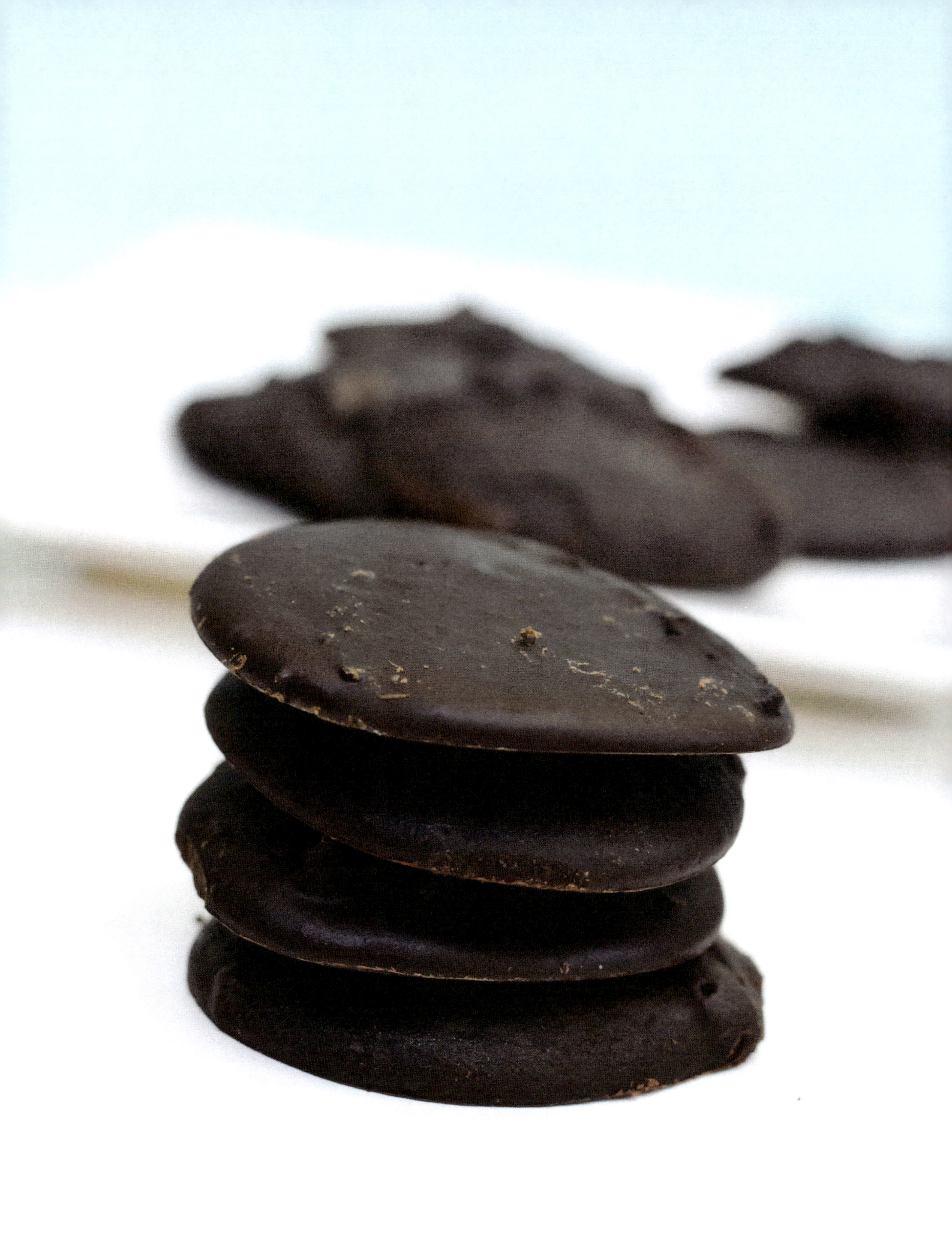

This recipe was a life changer for us and for the blogging community. We are so pleased with it and think you will be to as many of you have already told us how much you adore them! We have a few variations of this recipe on our blog, so make sure you check them out. Plus we have a video of Michelle making them on our YouTube channel (pure2rawtwins).

Healthy thin mint cookie packed with protein!

PROTEIN THIN MINTS

Ingredients:
3/4 cup hemp protein powder (3oz)
1/2 cup + 2 tablespoons cacao powder (2 1/2oz)
1 teaspoon vanilla extract
1/2 teaspoon stevia, liquid
1 teaspoon peppermint extract
about 6 tablespoons coconut oil, liquid (3oz)

MAKES ABOUT 9 COOKIES

In a large bowl place cacao powder and hemp protein powder. Stir together. Next add in vanilla, peppermint extract and liquid stevia. Then add in coconut oil slowly one tablespoon at a time.

Add more or less oil depending on what thickness of thin mint you want. We found 3oz of coconut oil was perfect. This recipe is heat sensitive due to coconut oil.

Substitutions:
Any protein powder can be used instead of the hemp protein, just be aware each will have a different flavor and provide a slightly different texture. Adjust coconut oil and sweetness ratios accordingly.
Carob powder can be used instead of cacao; you might need to increase the coconut oil as carob can be thicker than cacao.
Cacao butter can be used instead of coconut oil.
Any extract flavor can be used for the mint extract.

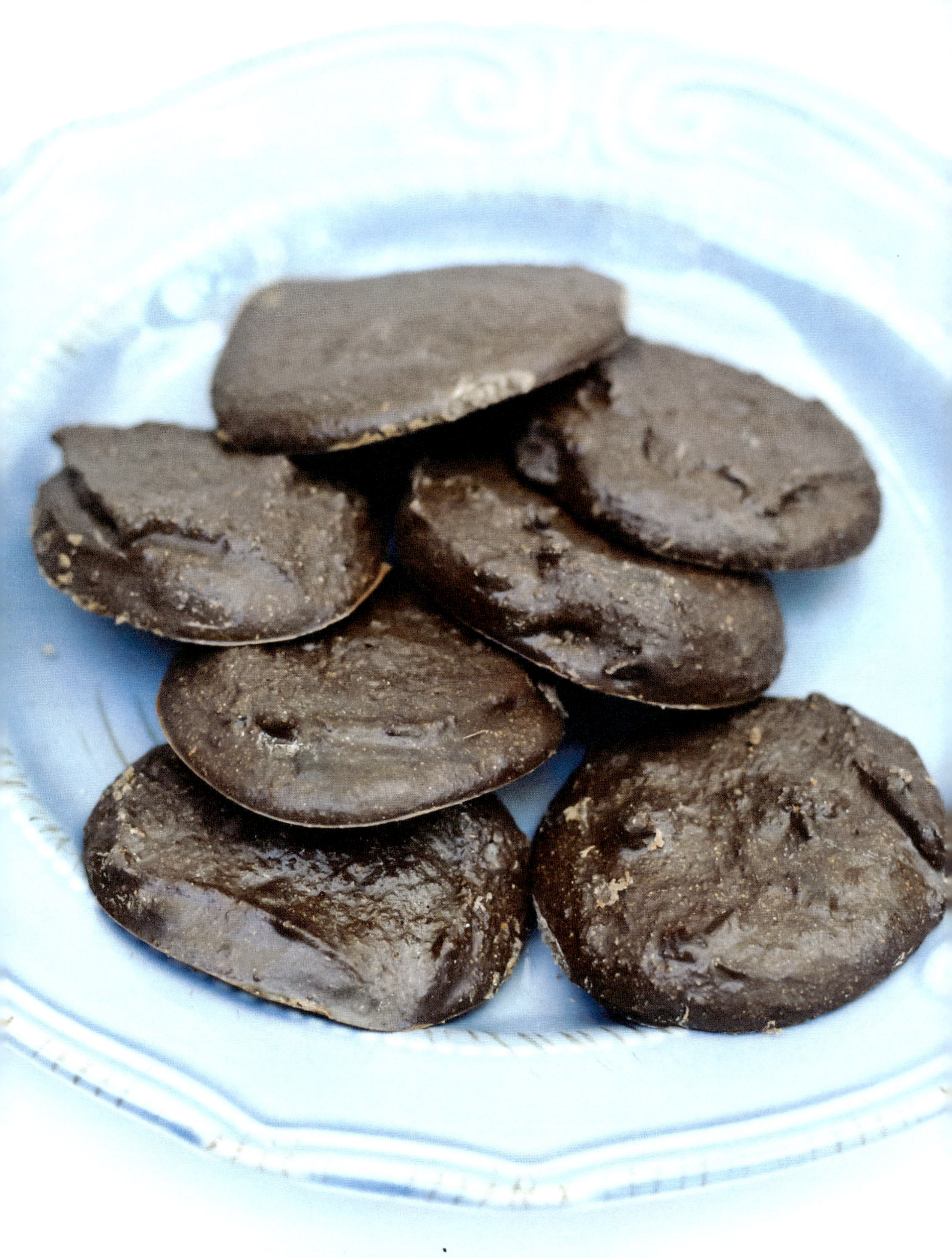

Here is our non-protein powder based thin mint cookie. We received lots of requests for it and we are so excited about this version. Coconut flour is a key ingredient; it's also a great source of fiber! Due to the coconut flour this thin mint version has a slightly different mint flavor but still delicious!

Melt-in-your-mouth chocolate mint cookie.

COCO THIN MINTS

Ingredients:
1/4 cup store bought coconut flour (1oz)
1/4 cup + 2 tbsp cacao powder (1oz)
1/4 cup mesquite (1 1/4oz)
1 teaspoon vanilla extract
1/2 teaspoon stevia, liquid
1 teaspoon peppermint extract
5 tablespoons coconut oil, liquid (2 1/2 oz)

MAKES 9 COOKIES

In a large bowl place cacao powder, mesquite, and coconut flour (store bought). Stir together. Next add in vanilla, peppermint extract and liquid stevia. Then add in your coconut oil slowly one tablespoon at a time.

Add more or less oil depending on what thickness thin mint you want.

We found 2 1/2 of coconut oil was perfect. This recipe is heat sensitive due to the coconut oil.

Substitutions:
Carob powder can be used instead of cacao; you might need to increase the coconut oil as carob can be thicker than cacao.
Cacao butter can be used instead of coconut oil.
Any extract flavor can be used for the mint extract.
For the coconut flour in this recipe, works the best with store bought.

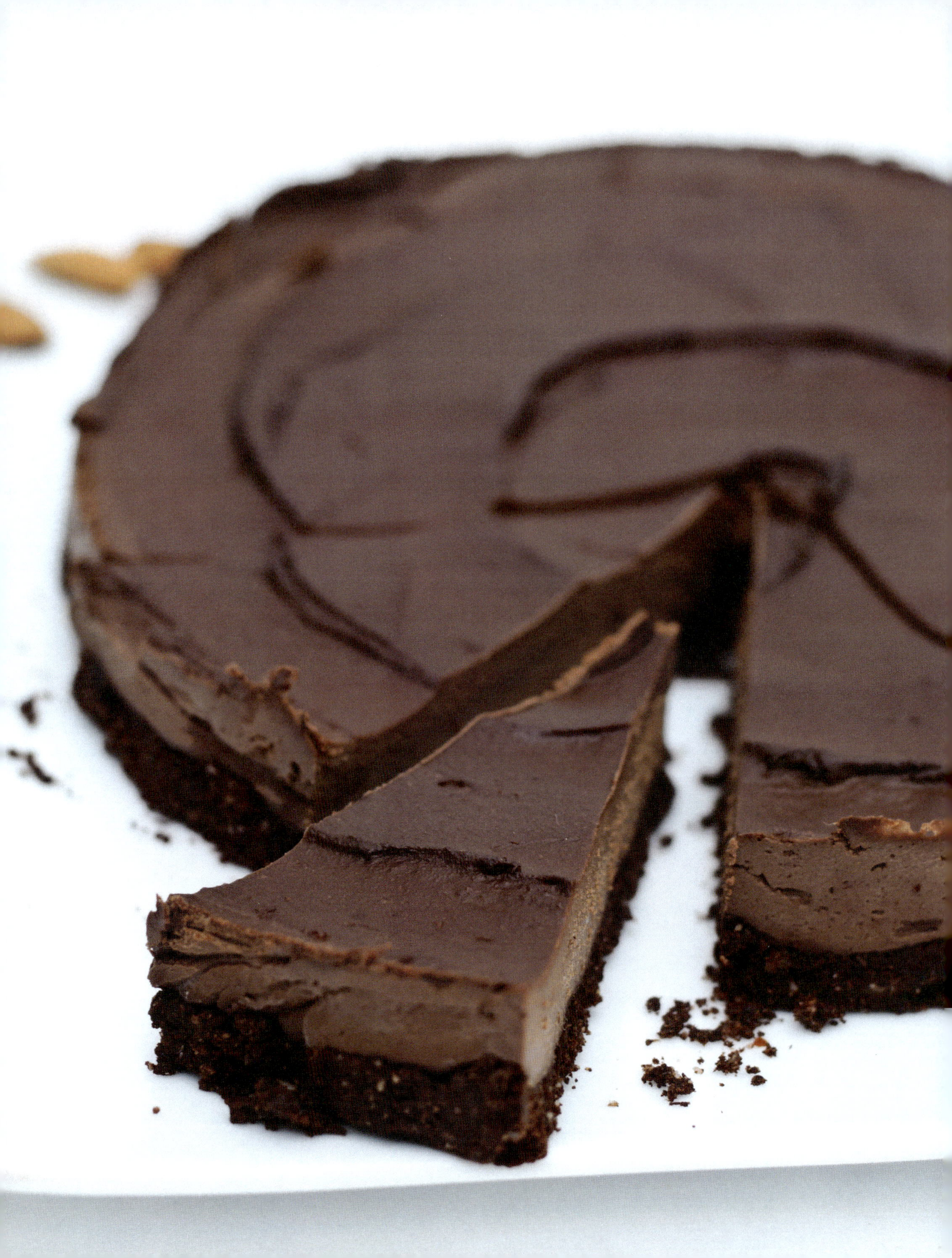

Hands down the BEST dairy- free cheesecake. One of our most popular recipes to date from our blog. Always our go-to dessert to please anyone! It is our never fail dessert recipe. We also have a video of Lori making this on our YouTube channel.

Chocolate heaven on a plate!

CHOCOLATE CREAM CAKE

Crust Ingredients:
1 cup purelytwins almond flour (4oz)
1/2 cup cacao powder (1 1/2oz)
3-4 medjool dates (1 1/2-2oz)
1 teaspoon vanilla extract
pinch sea salt

Cream Filling:
3/4 cup cacao powder (3 1/4oz)
2 cups cashew pieces (11 1/2oz dry cashews)
1/2 cup coconut oil, liquid (4oz)
1/2 cup maple syrup
2 teaspoons vanilla extract
1/2 cup water

MAKES ONE 9 INCH CAKE

First make crust by placing all ingredients into food processor and begin pulsing. We recommend soaking dates for 1-2 minutes before blending, this makes them easier to blend. Once crust is made place into the 9 inch springform pan (we recommend this pan to make it easy to remove and cut). Press crust into pan. We line our pan with wax paper, making it easier to remove crust once done. Next make your filling.

We recommend soaking cashews for at least an hour for easy blending. Rinse well. Place cashews, maple syrup, vanilla, and water into blender. Start to blend. Next add in raw cacao powder. Blend some more. Wiping down sides when needed.

End with adding coconut oil. It is best if everything is at room temperature because coconut oil is sensitive to cold, and could get chunky. If that happens warm up water a little before pouring into blender. Blend until everything is nice and creamy.

Pour filling on top of crust. Smooth out with a spoon. Place in freezer to set for about 4-6 hours.
Then store cake in fridge and enjoy chilled or at room temperatue.

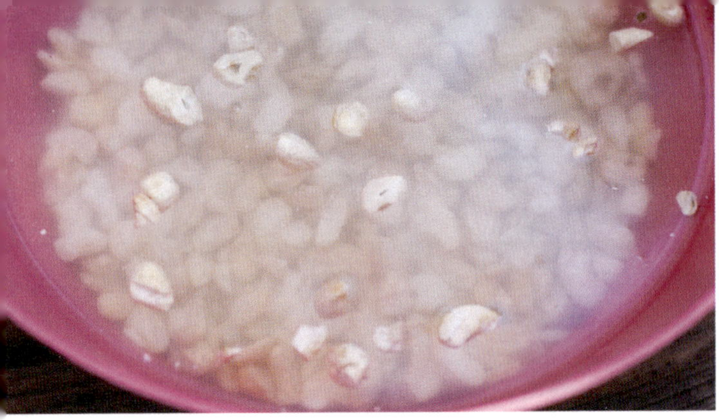
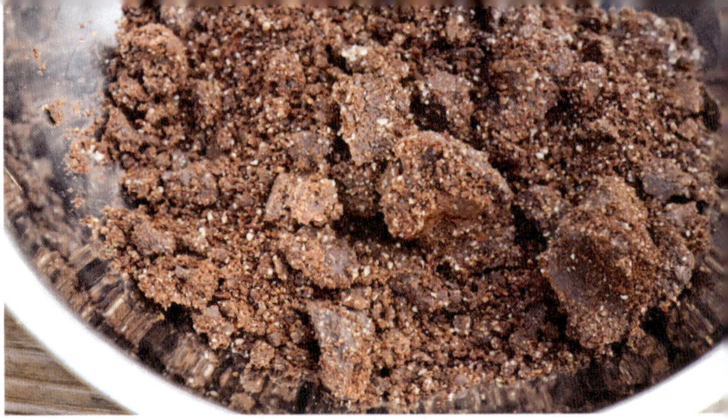
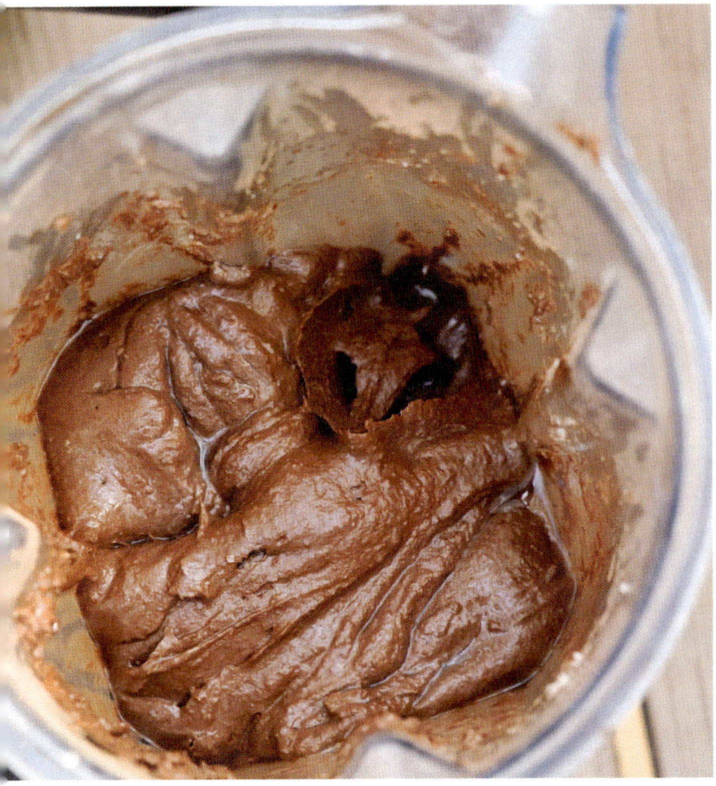
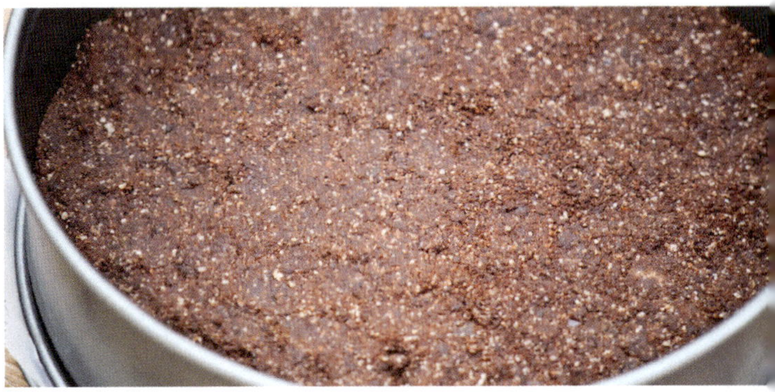
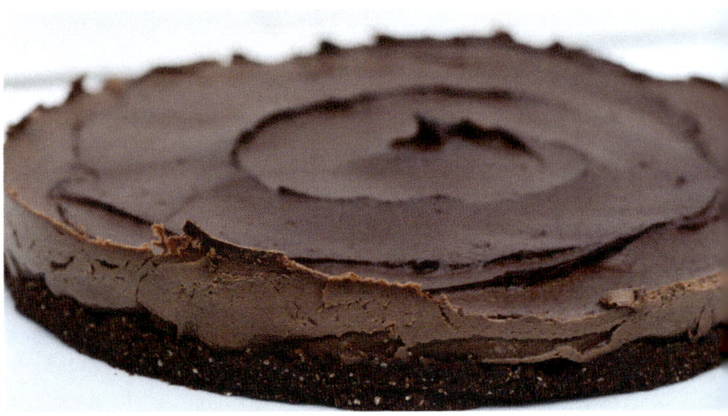
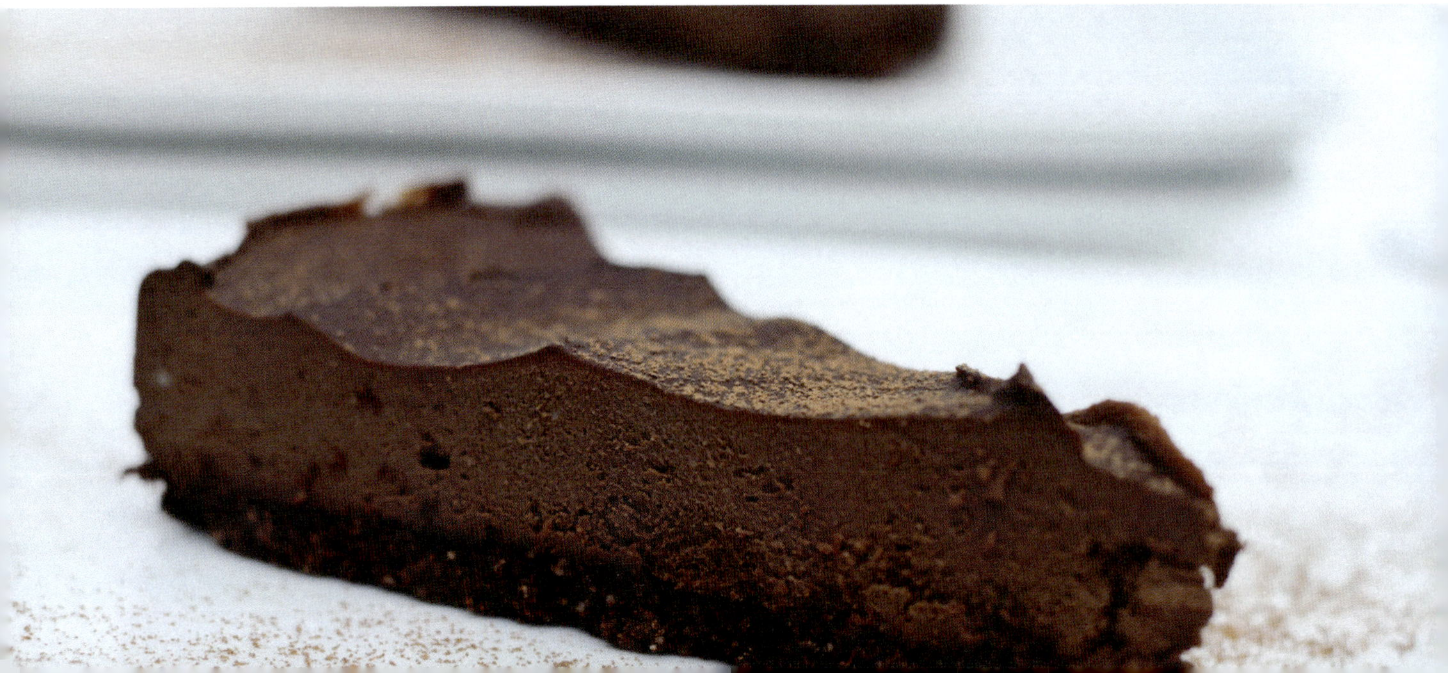

TIPS AND SUBSTITUTIONS

We recommend soaking the cashews to help provide a rich creamy texture and helps with digestion. Make sure you rinse your cashews well before using. Macadamia nuts are the next best option and almond would be a third if you cannot have cashews.
The batter will get thick in blender (best if you have a high speed blender like a Vita-mix). Just take your time with it.
For the maple syrup, can use honey, agave, or coconut nectar.
For the crust, pecans are a good substitute for the almonds.
Instead of dates you could use another liquid sweetner like maple syrup. Start small and add 1 tbsp at a time.

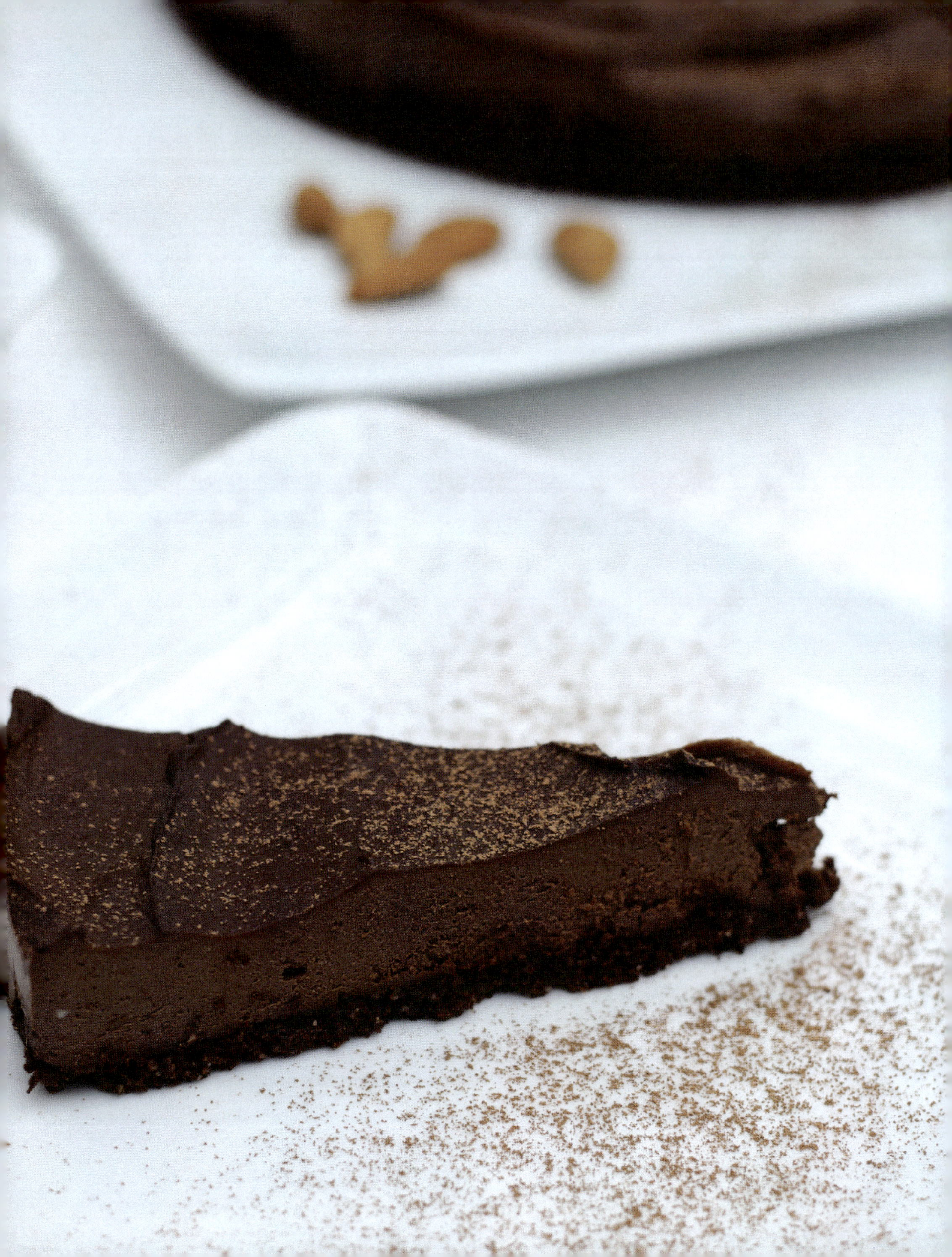

Since our original chocolate cream cake was such a hit we knew we had to make a low-sugar version. This cream cake is just as delicious as the original! Perfect for those who like stevia or are watching their sugar.

Dense not too sweet dark chocolate cream cake.

LOW-SUGAR CHOCOLATE CREAM CAKE

Crust Ingredients:
1 cup purelytwins almond flour (4oz)
1/2 cup cacao powder (1 1/2oz)
3-4 medjool dates (1 1/2-2oz)
1 teaspoon vanilla extract
pinch sea salt

Cream Filling:
3/4 cup cacao powder (3 1/4oz)
2 1/4 cups cashew pieces (11 1/2oz dry cashews)
1/2 cup coconut oil, liquid (4oz)
3/4 teaspoon liquid stevia
2 teaspoons vanilla extract
1/2 cup + 2 tbsp water

MAKES ONE 9 INCH CAKE

First make crust by placing all ingredients into food processor and begin pulsing. We recommend soaking dates for 1-2 minutes before blending, this makes them easier to blend. Once crust is made place into the 9 inch springform pan (we recommend this pan to make it easy to remove and cut). Press crust into pan. We line our pan with wax paper, making it easier to remove crust once done. Next make your filling.

We recommend soaking cashews for at least an hour for easy blending. Rinse well. Place cashews, stevia, vanilla, and water into blender. Start to blend. Next add in raw cacao powder. Blend some more. Wiping down sides when needed.

End with adding coconut oil. It is best if everything is at room temperature because coconut oil is sensitive to cold, and could get chunky. If that happens warm up water a little before pouring into blender. Blend until everything is nice and creamy. Filling will be thick!

Pour filling on top of crust. Smooth out with a spoon. Place in freezer to set for about 4-6 hours.
Then store cake in fridge and enjoy chilled or at room temperatue.

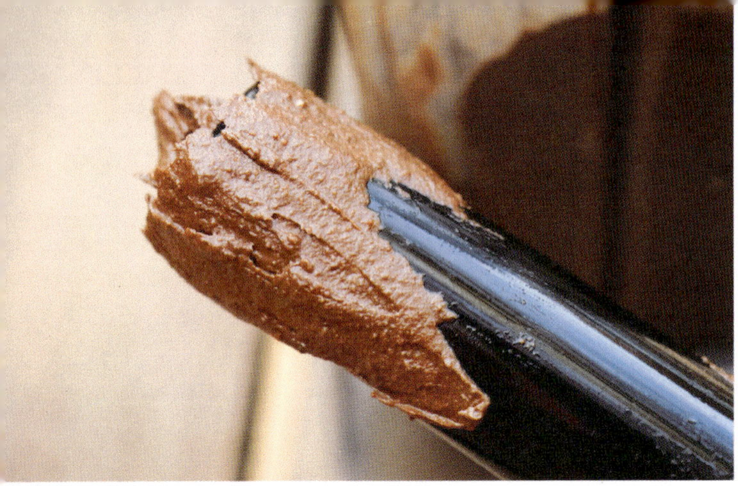
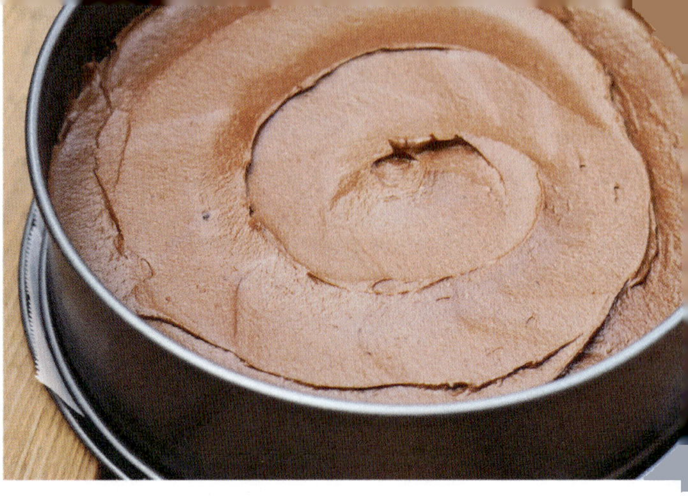
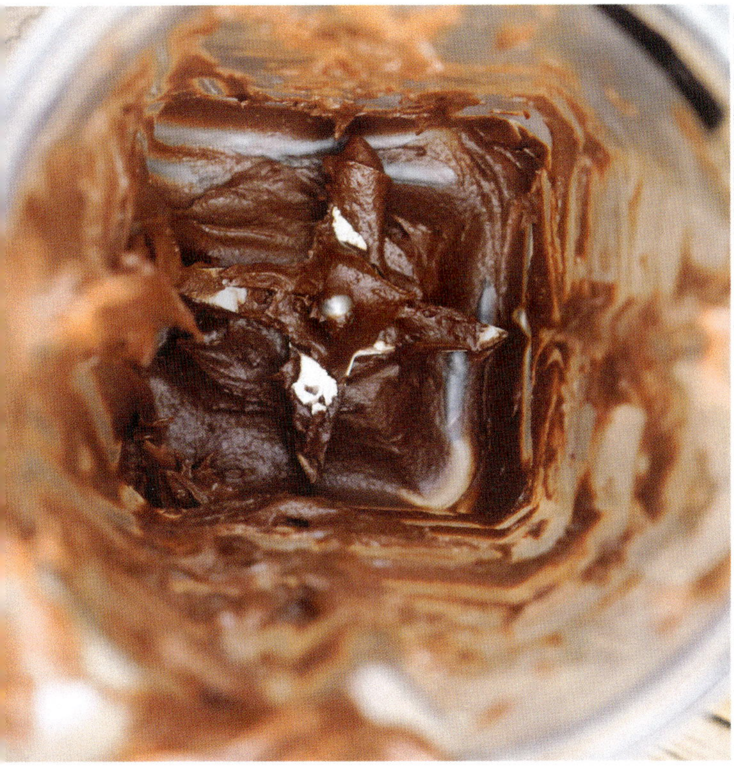
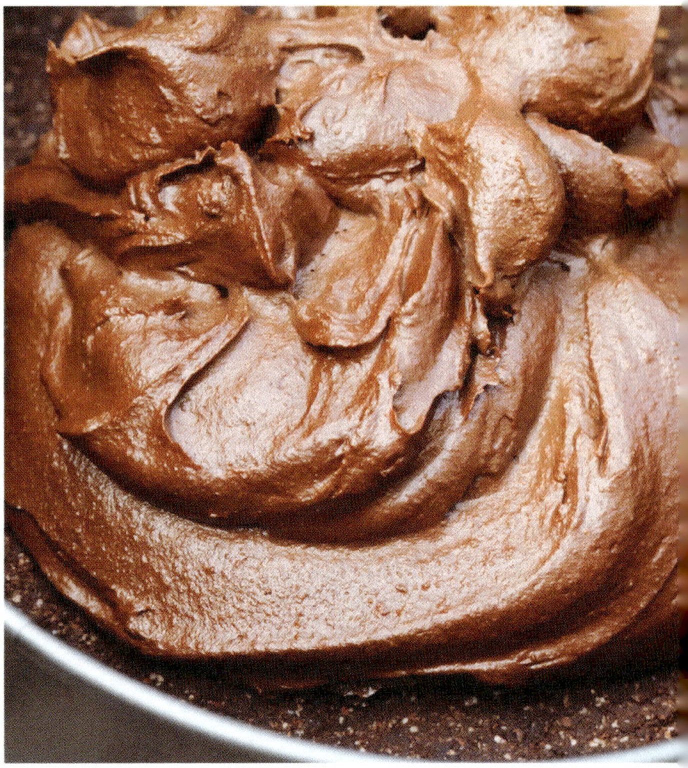
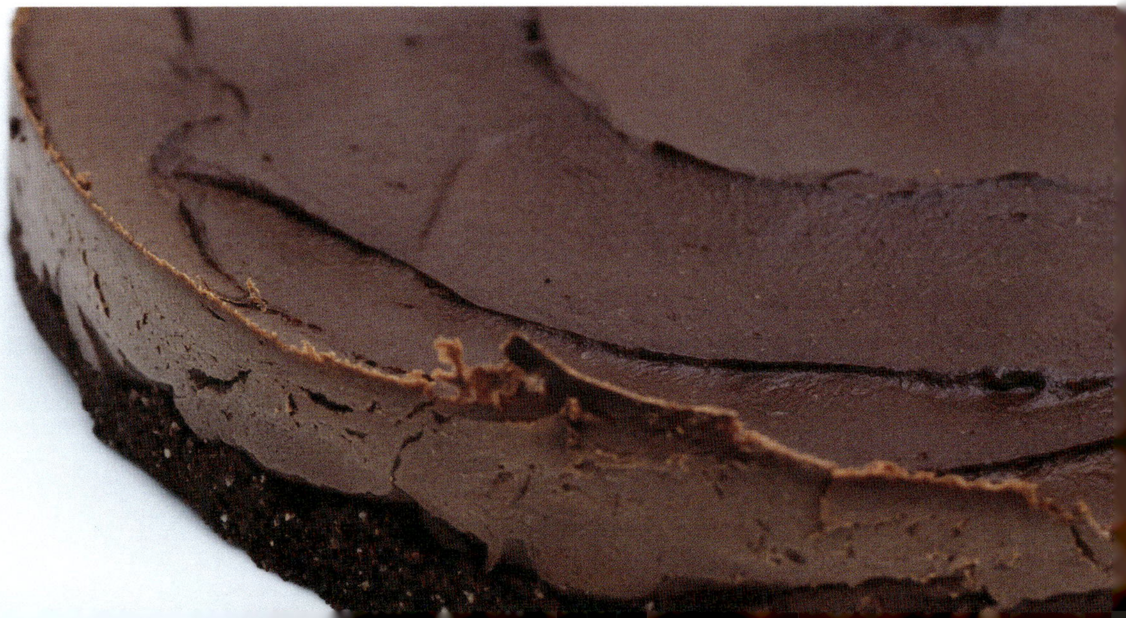

TIPS AND SUBSTITUTIONS

We recommend soaking the nuts to help provide a rich creamy texture.
Make sure you rinse your cashews well before using.
Macadamia nuts are the next best option, as almond would be third.
The batter will get thick in blender (best if you have a high speed blender like a Vitamix). Just take your time with it.
You can use powered stevia if desired, start small and adjust sweetness accordingly. We prefer the flavor of liquid stevia.
For the crust, you could use pecans as a good substitute for the almonds.
Instead of dates you could use another liquid sweener like coconut nectar to keep it low in sugar all together. Start small and add 1 tbsp at a time.

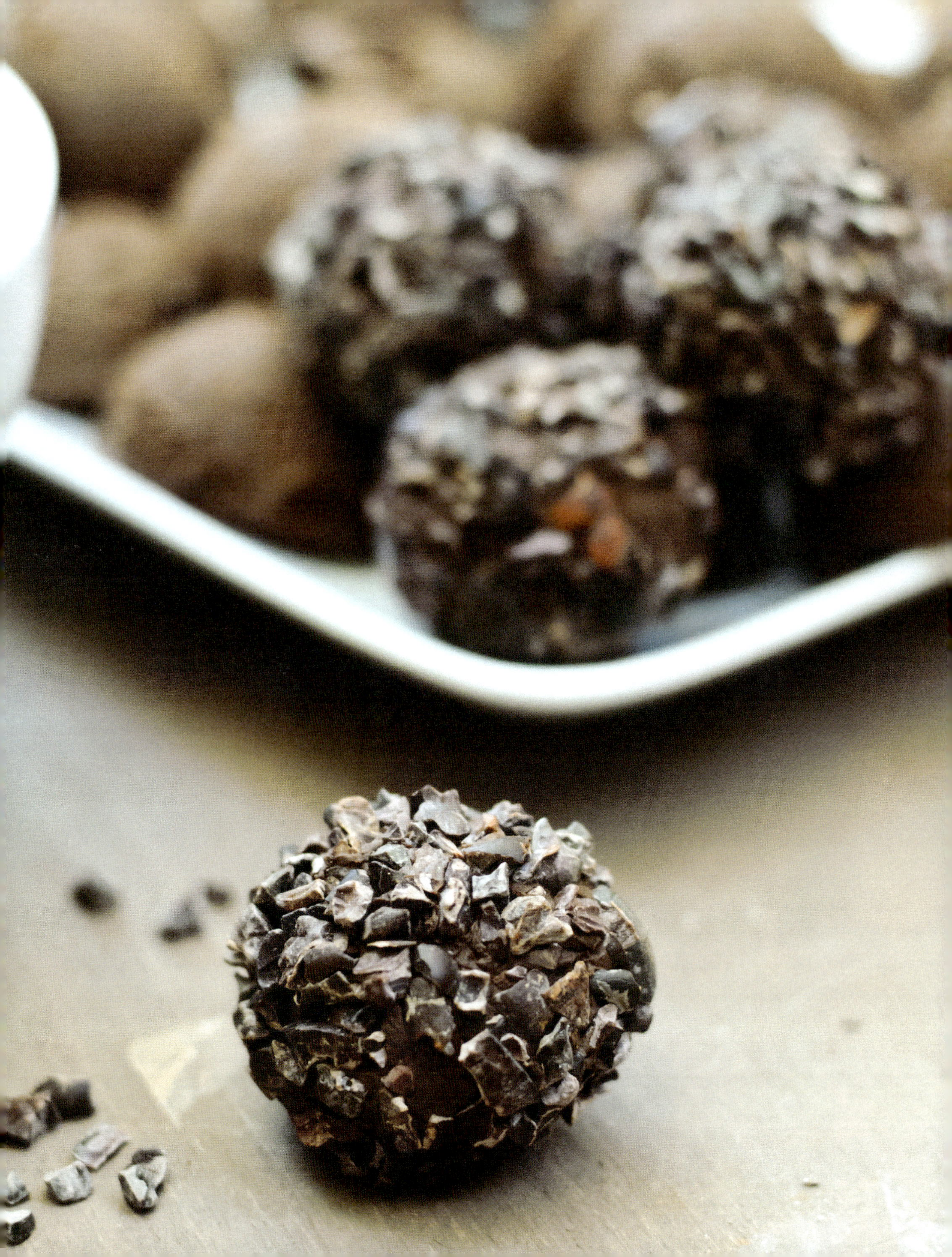

Between this recipe and our chocolate cream cake it is a hard battle as to which recipe is our ultimate favorite, as we swoon over both! The perfect blend of dark chocolate with a hint of sweetness. Even with the addition of hemp for a more protein-packed truffle these little guys are a life changer!

Hands down the best chocolate truffle ever!

CHOCOLATE PROTEIN TRUFFLES

Ingredients:
1 1/2 cups cacao powder (5oz)
1/2 cup + 2 tablespoons hemp protein (2 1/2oz)
1/4 teaspoons sea salt
1 tablespoon vanilla extract
2 tablespoons coconut oil, liquid (1oz)
2 tablespoons coconut butter, softened (1 1/4oz)
1/2 cup coconut nectar (6oz)
1 cup melted cacao butter (8oz)

ABOUT 30 TRUFFLES, WE DO NOT HAVE AN ACCURATE COUNT AS WE EAT THEM AS WE SCOOP

In a very large deep glass bowl place cacao powder, hemp protein powder, sea salt, and vanilla. Stir together. Next add in coconut butter. We recommend softening it for easier stirring. Add in coconut nectar and melted cacao butter. Stir with a whisk, as it will help mix it all together. Whisk until clumps are gone. End with stirring in liquid coconut oil. Continue to stir until everything is blended together.

Let sit at room temperature for about 4-5 hours, or until firm to touch. Then scoop with a cookie scooper. May leave as is, or roll into a ball to coat with toppings.

Amount of truffles will depend on size scooper and amount consume during production.

Options to coat:
Cacao nibs, ground nuts, coconut flakes, or dip in melted chocolate morsels.

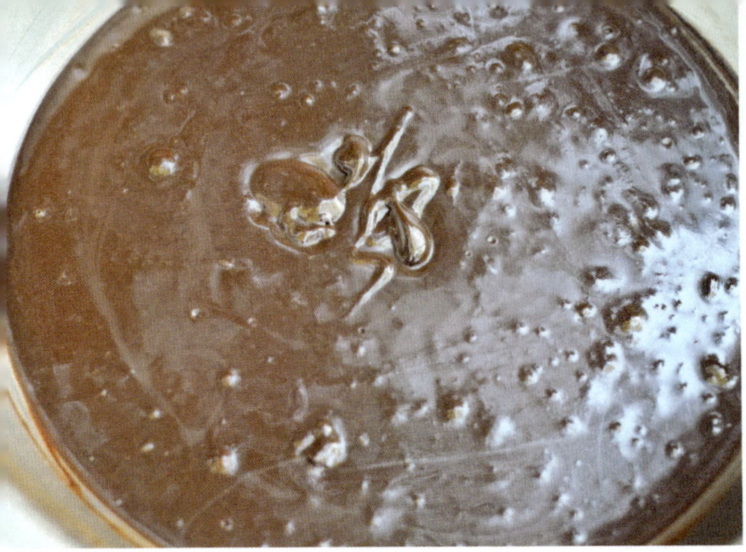
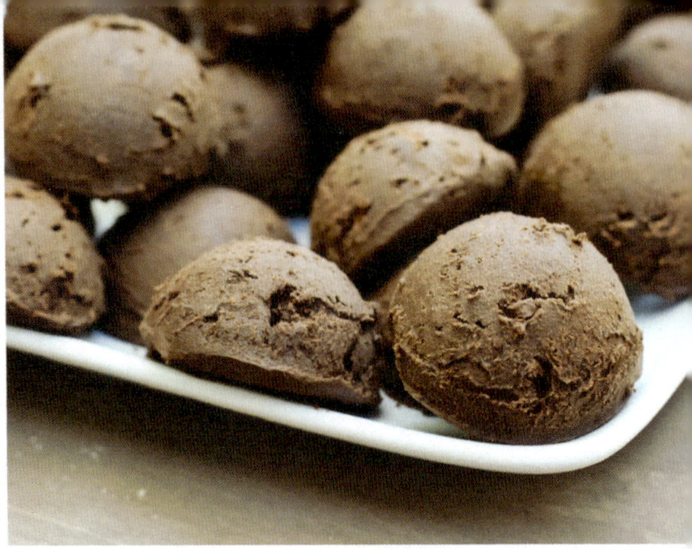
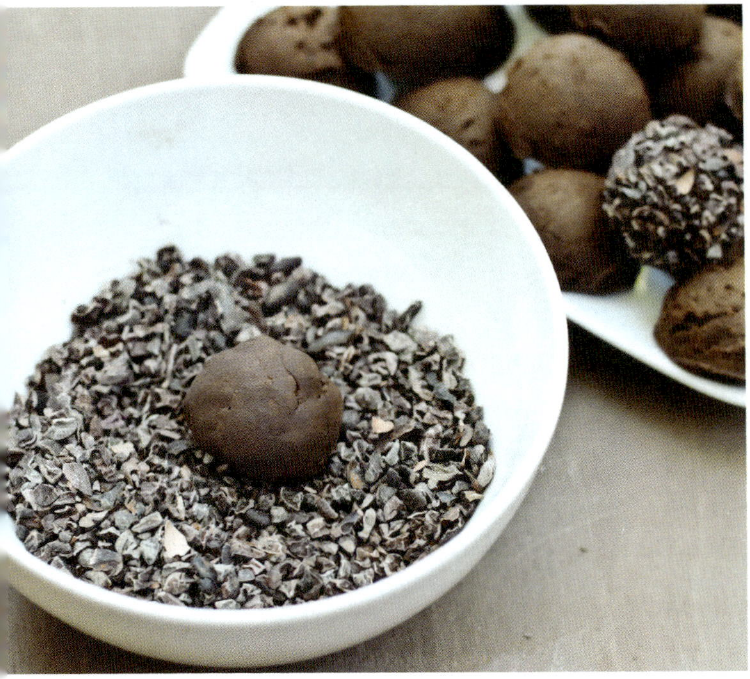
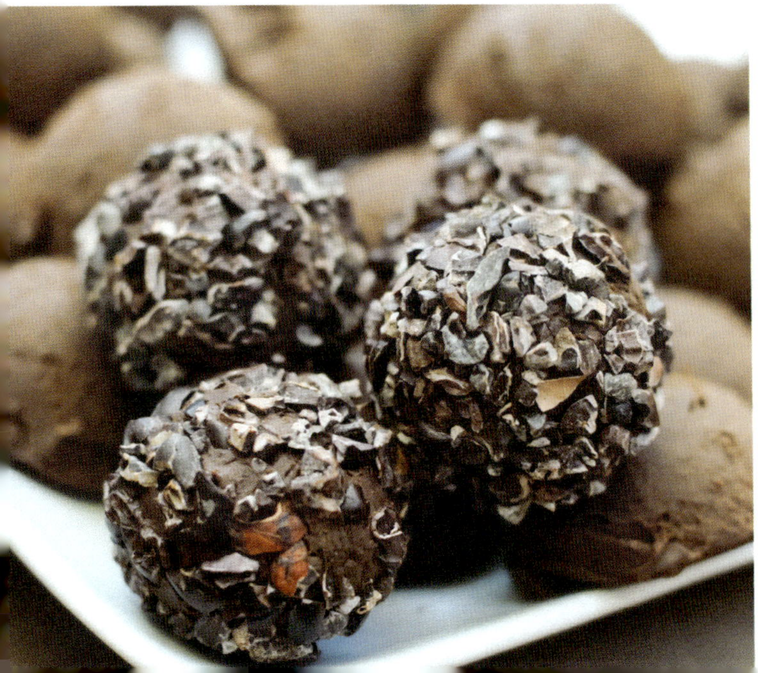
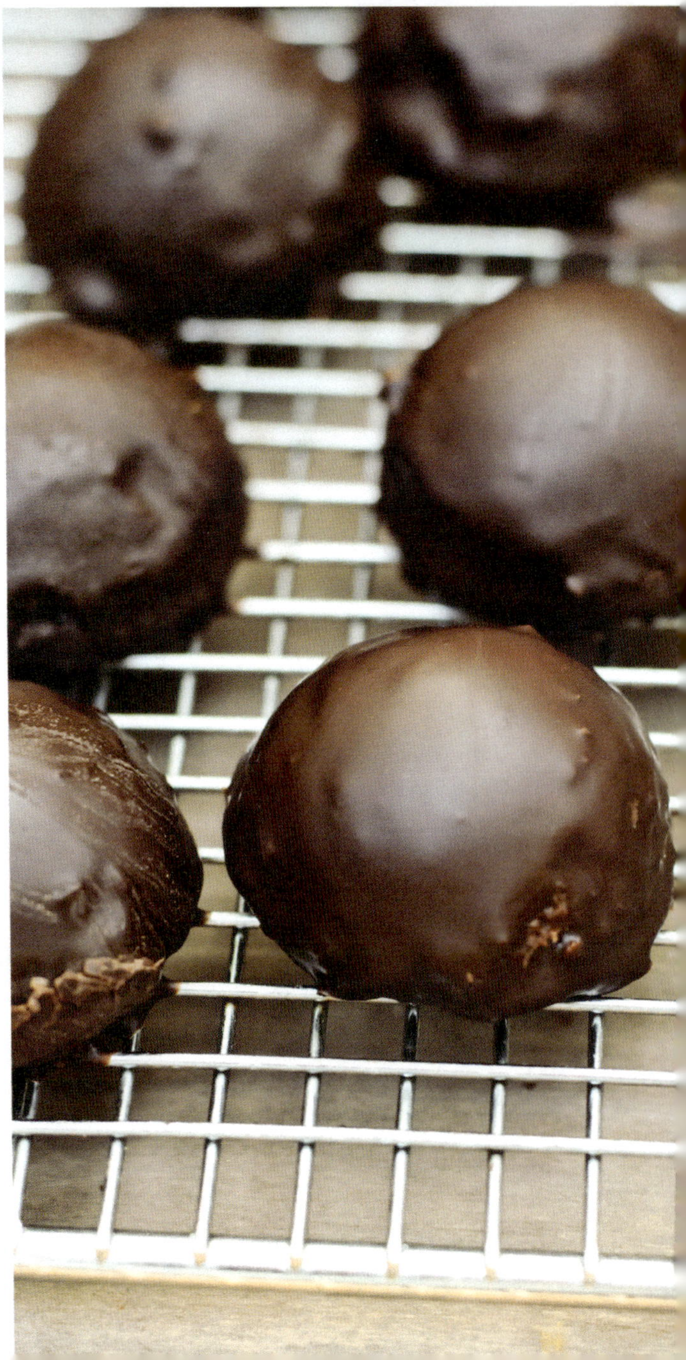

TIPS AND SUBSTITUTIONS

Any protein powder will work to replace hemp protein. Just remember the final flavor and texture may vary.

Lucuma or carob powder can be used instead of protein powder.

We have made a version without protein powder and coconut butter and leaving rest of the ingredients the same. And it came out great!

Any liquid sweetener (honey, maple or agave) can be used to replace the coconut nectar.

Please make sure your liquid ingredients are soft in liquid form!

These can be made days in advance before enjoying!

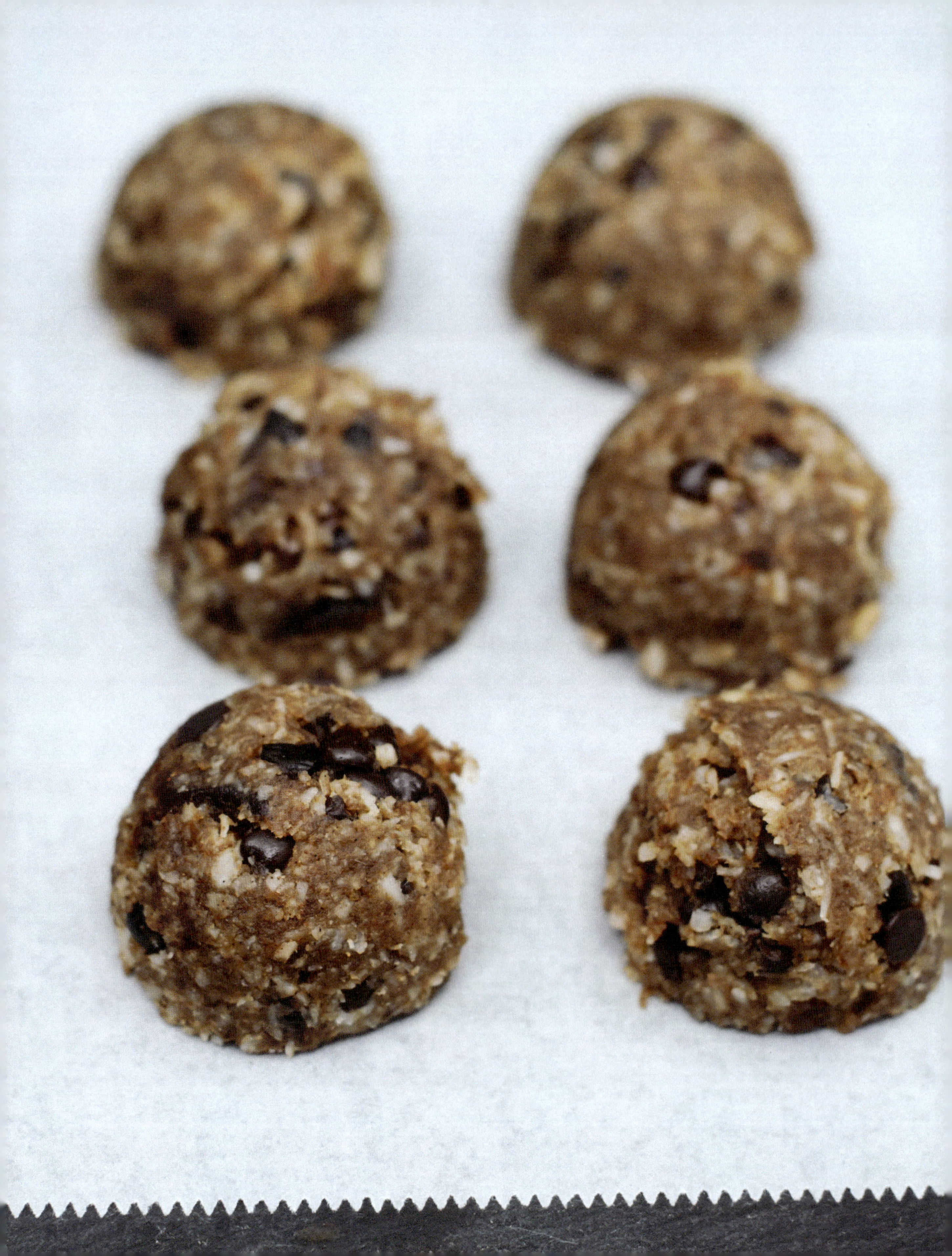

Another great way we love to enjoy raw cookies. We adore the unique chew that the coconut flakes give to these raw cookies. These can be dehydrated for a warm raw cookie if you desire that will melt-in-your mouth. The mesquite and dates add a smooth rich caramel-like flavor that makes them irresistible.

Never enough raw cookies around.

RAW CHOCOLATE CHIP COOKIES

Ingredients:
- 1/2 cup purelytwins coconut flakes (1 1/2oz)
- 1/4 cup purelytwins cashew flour (1oz)
- 1 tablespoon mesquite (1/4oz)
- 2 teaspoons vanilla extract
- 2 tablespoons coconut butter (1 1/4oz)
- 2-3 medjool dates, pitted (1oz)
- 2 tablespoons chocolate chips
- 1 tablespoon water

Makes 8-9 cookies

Make cashew flour (p.43) and coconut flour (p.44). You can either make these cookies in blender like a Vita-mix or in a food processor. Place all ingredients into blender, except the chocolate chips.

Pulse until everything comes together. Then in a large bowl place cookie batter and stir in chocolate chips. Batter should come together easily to scoop into cookie shapes.

Amount of cookies will vary depending on size scooper used. Recommend storing in refrigerator or freezer. Enjoy at room temperature.

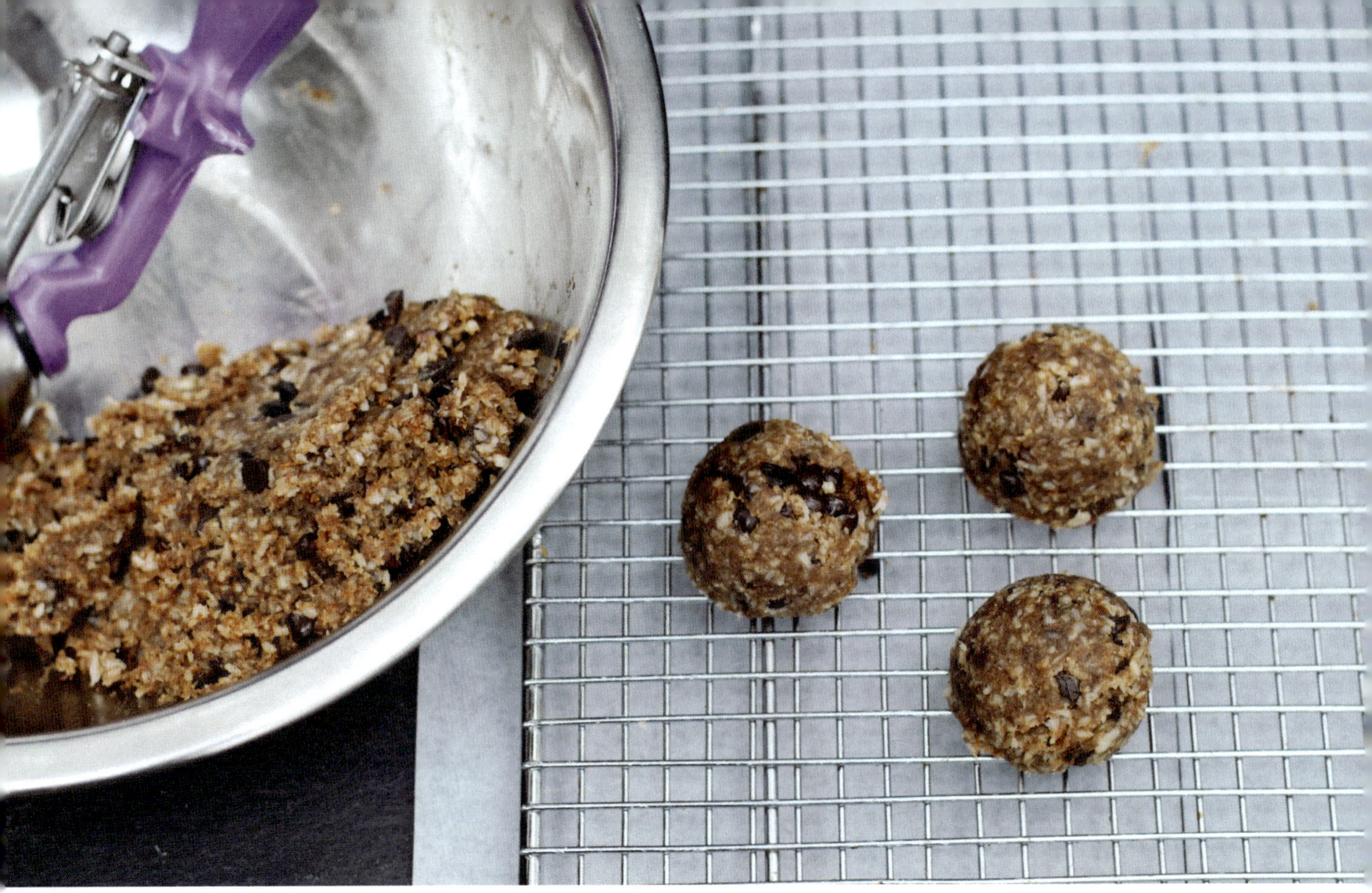

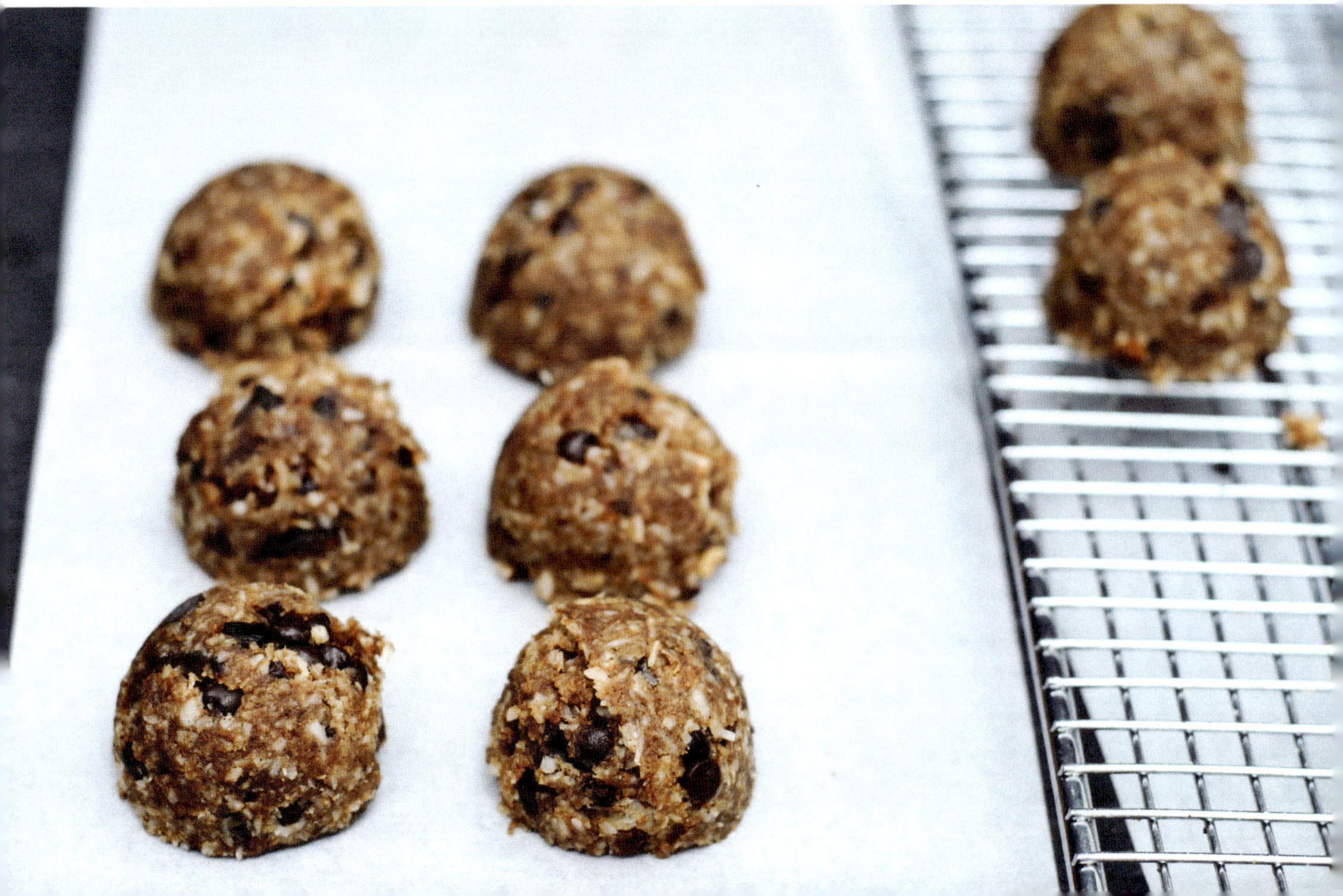

TIPS AND SUBSTITUTIONS

Any nut flour can be used for the cashews and/or coconut flakes. We like to use coconut flakes because it helps reduce the amount of nuts used. Plus we just love coconut.
You can leave coconut flakes whole creating a chewier cookie.
Cacao nibs can be used for the chocolate chips or a combination of the two.
Mesquites provides more depth in flavor, but can be omitted.
Only add in water if your batter is really dry.
We recommend soaking your dates for a little bit in water to help make them easier to blend. Add more or less to get your desired sweetness.

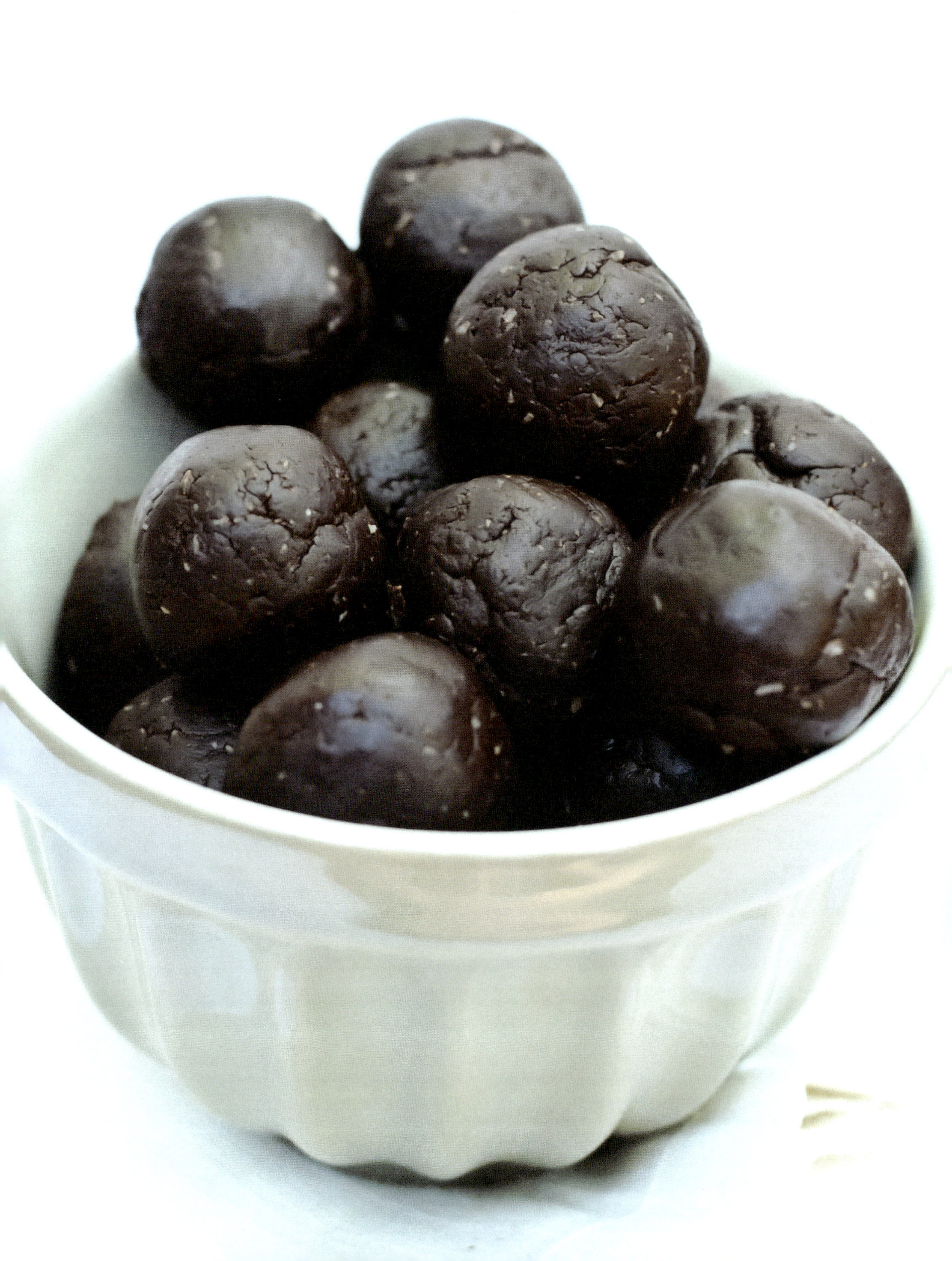

This raw brownie can be a little sticky to work with, but worth it in the end. Especially for rich dark chocolate lovers like us. You can add any flavoring of your liking to this basic recipe! The possibilites are endless. Coconut nectar provides such an unique chew to this raw brownie. Perfect snack for traveling.

Chewy dark chocolate brownie..

RAW CHEWY BROWNIE BITES

Ingredients:
1/4 cup purelytwins coconut flour (1oz)
1/4 cup lucuma (1 1/4oz)
1 1/2 cup cacao (5oz)
2 tablespoons coconut butter (1 1/2oz)
6-7 tablespoons coconut nectar (4 1/2oz)

makes 20 brownie bites

First make coconut flour (p.44)
Next place all dry ingredients into a large bowl and stir together. Then start adding in wet ingredients (coconut butter and coconut nectar). Continue to stir.

Might have to use hands as it is a **very** thick and sticky batter. Food grade gloves can make it easier to work with. Scoop with cookie scooper or spoon.

May eat as is or dehydrate at 110 degrees for 1-2 hours for a warm brownie bite. Store in refrigerator. Enjoy at room temperature.

Substitutions:
If you do not have lucuma or purelytwins coconut flour, you can use a purelytwins nut flour.
Coconut oil can be used instead of coconut butter. Be warned it will have a harder texture when chilled.
Maple syrup or honey can be used instead of coconut nectar. Maple syrup will
provide a little less chew texture and more sweetness.
Can use protein powder, carob, or mesquite instead of lucuma.
Other flavor ideas: 1 1/2 tsp cardamom or cinnamon; 1/2-1 tsp mint, almond or coconut extract; pinch of cayenne for heat.
You can try making them in blender or food processor but since batter is really thick it might be difficult to blend well.

CREAMY CASHEW FROSTING

This is our go-to basic frosting. Cashews make the perfect creamy dairy-free frosting mixed with some coconut butter, even coconut oil would be delicious. The possibilites with this basic frosting are endless. We have a few variations of our frostings on our blog (*purelytwins.com*).

Ingredients:
1 1/4 cups raw cashew pieces
2 tablespoons coconut butter, softened (1 1/4oz)
2-3 teaspoons vanilla extract
6-7 tablespoons water
25-30 drops stevia, liquid

MAKES ABOUT 1 1/4 CUPS FROSTING

Soak cashews for at least 1 hour. This make them easier to blend. Once cashews are soaked, rinse well. Place cashews in blender with coconut butter, vanilla, and stevia. Start to blend. Take breaks and wipe down sides and continue blending. Add in water one tablespoon at a time until you get the desired thickness.

If you want to use a liquid sweetener (maple syrup, honey, agave) we suggest reducing the water by 1-3 tbsp.

Chocolate Frosting

This is our go-to basic chocolate frosting. Avocados make the perfect creamy dairy-free frosting. Mix them with some cacao powder and coconut oil and you have one amazing frosting. The possibilites with this basic chocolate frosting are endless. We have a few variations of our frostings on our blog (*purelytwins.com*).

Ingredients:
1 Hass avocado, large
3 tablespoons raw cacao powder
1-2 teaspoons vanilla extract
2 tablespons coconut oil
20-30 drops stevia, liquid

MAKES ABOUT 1 1/4 CUPS FROSTING

Cut open avocado and remove pit. Scoop out avocado and place in high powered blender along with your cacao powder, coconut oil, vanilla, and stevia. Start to blend. Take breaks and wipe down sides and continue blending. Keep blending until you get a smooth creamy texture.

If you want to use a liquid sweetener (maple syrup, honey, agave) we suggest 3 tbsp coconut oil to make sure it gets hard and easy to work with.

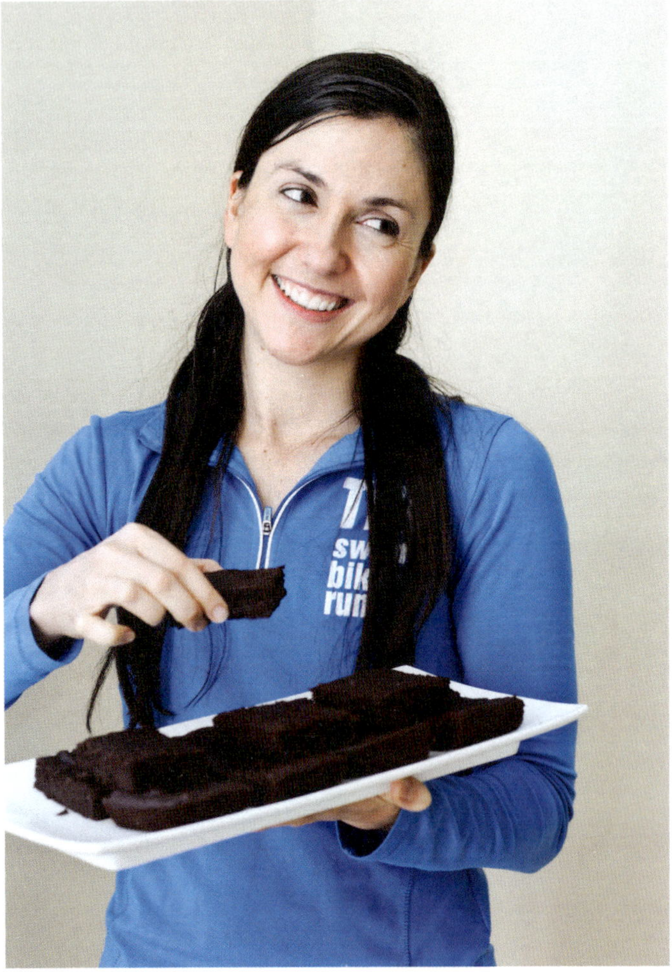

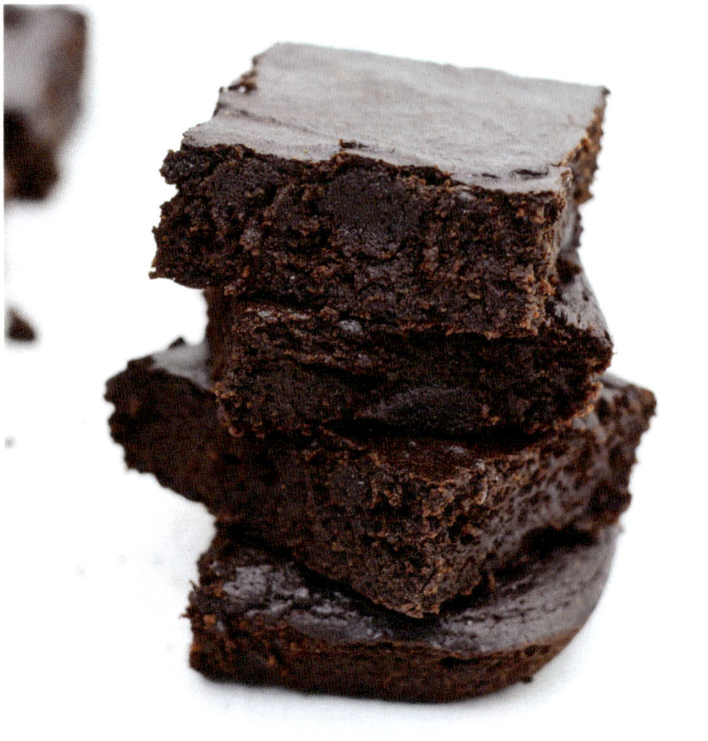

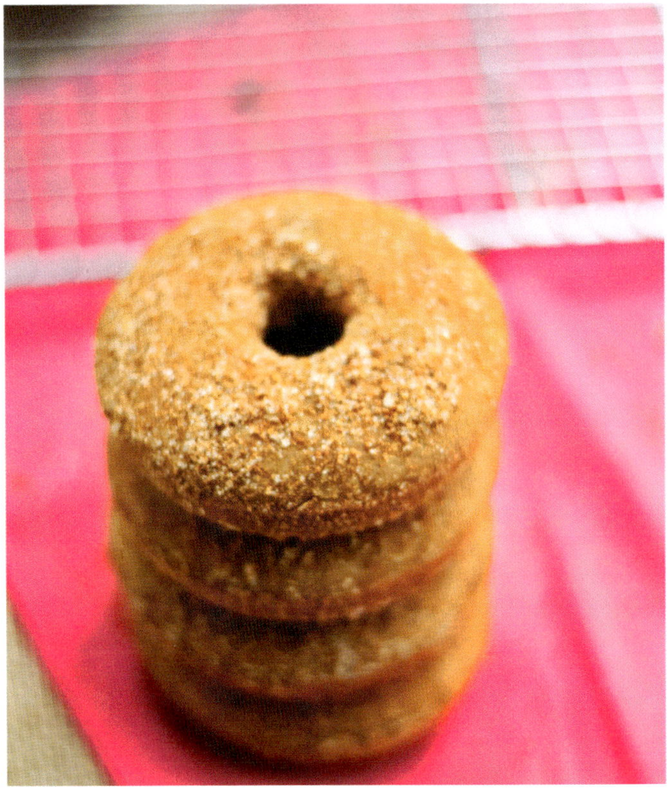

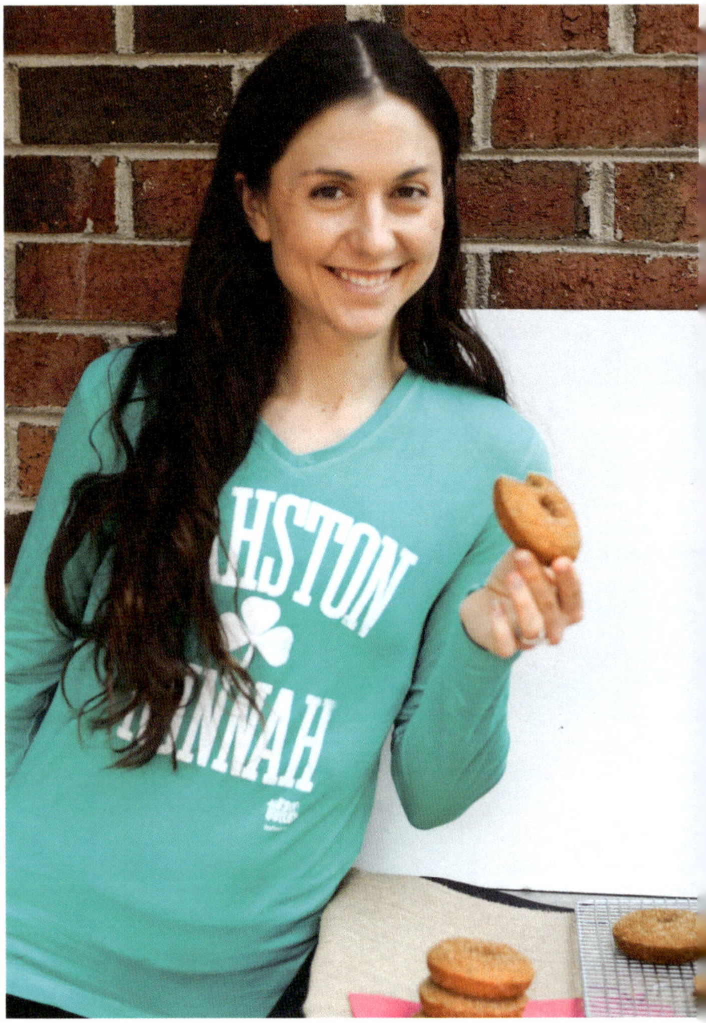

MORE THOUGHTS ABOUT SUBSTITUTIONS

We provide substitutions for each recipe, but keep in mind we have worked really hard to perfect these recipes from texture to flavor. Recipe development can be tricky as it takes time to find the perfect balance of everything. We wanted recipes that taste amazing!

NOTE: Altering just one ingredient may change the final outcome of the recipe. But we encourage you to experiment in your own kitchen.

Now go make a mess in the kitchen!

Pearly Twins

Resources

Recommended brands and where to buy the ingredients used in our recipes.

Raw organic cold-pressed coconut oil: Nutiva- http://nutiva.com or Wilderness Family Naturals- http://www.wildernessfamilynaturals.com
Raw coconut butter: Artisana- http://www.artisanafoods.com or make it homemade (see our blog *purelytwins.com* for how we make it)
Raw coconut flakes: Ultimate Superfoods-http://www.ultimatesuperfoods.com/ or Blue Mountain Organics- http://bluemountainorganics.com/
Medjool dates: raw medjool dates can be found online or most health food stores
Raw cacao: Navitas Naturals- http://www.navitasnaturals.com or Ultimate Superfoods- http://www.ultimatesuperfoods.com/
For raw nuts: Blue Mountain Organics- http://bluemountainorganics.com/ or health food stores
Coconut sugar: Navitas Naturals- http://www.navitasnaturals.com or Ultimate Superfoods- http://www.ultimatesuperfoods.com
Coconut nectar: Coconut Secret- http://coconutsecret.com/ (and coconut flour)
Grade B Maple syrup: we try to find local or use organic from health food stores
Liquid Stevia: Sweet Leaf- http://www.sweetleaf.com/products/sweet-drops-products or NuNaturals- https://nunaturals.com/
Mesquite and lucuma powders: Navitas Naturals- http://www.navitasnaturals.com or Ultimate Superfoods- http://www.ultimatesuperfoods.com

Mountain Rose Herbs: Great website for buying spices, sea salt, vanilla in bulk http://www.mountainroseherbs.com/
Bob's Red Mill: The brand we like for our gluten-free flours (sorghum, brown rice, arrowroot starch, coconut flour)- http://www.bobsredmill.com

Dehydrator: Excalibur- http://www.excaliburdehydrator.com/
Blender: Vita-Mix- https://www.vitamix.com/Home/
Other tools you might need: donut pan (Norpro 6-count), springform, cookie scooper, 6-cavity bundt pan
Amazon: where you will find a great selection of the ingredients and tools we have listed here

ABOUT THE TWINS

Lori and Michelle are the creators of the blog *purelytwins.com,* chefs, authors, FitFluential Ambassadors and fitness enthusiats. Michelle was trained at the world-renowned Matthew Kenney Academy in the art of creating gourmet raw vegan cuisine. Lori is currently studying to be a personal trainer to take her love of fitness to the next level. With both of their passions being developing healthy recipes they have put together their classic favorites for you to enjoy in the comfort of your own kitchen.

Thank you and we hope you enjoy our recipes.

"We remember our first time baking gluten-free egg-free baked goods and having many failures. But those failures taught us what works and what does not. This helped define what we want our allergy friendly treats to be like."

~ MICHELLE AND LORI, THE PURELY TWINS

Made in the USA
San Bernardino, CA
29 January 2013